100 Days of Staying the Hell Home

in 2020

#HashtagsOfCovid19

Sheri White

100 Days of Staying
the Hell Home
in 2020

#HashtagsOfCovid19

Sheri White

FOREWORD

by Tom Zuba

Author of *Permission to Mourn* and *Becoming Radiant*

My neighbor, Sheri White, has become my friend. Sheri and her husband and their kids (well, now just one at home) live up the hill from me. They're the ones with the huge pool. The huge stainless-steel pool. With the rafts and the open invitation. And the outdoor Halloween decorations. And turkey bingo with real prizes. And the delicious Christmas cookies. And Valentine's Day cookies. And St. Patrick's Day cookies. Which make me think of St. Patrick's Day. St. Patrick's Day 2020.

The Illinois governor announced he was cancelling the Chicago St. Patrick's Day parade. No dyed green river. No green beer. No choruses of "Danny Boy." I was ticked-off like any good half-Irishman would be. We love our corned beef, cabbage and one more high-spirited chorus of "Danny Boy." I was certain this virus-thing would be over in a week. Maybe two. Certainly, by month's end.

But, as you know by now, it went on. And on. And on and on and on. This Covid-thing went on. And every life was touched. Every. Single. Life. On. The. Planet.

Sheri saw the world, the one touched by Covid, as she is. Funny, generous, kind, caring, thoughtful and a lover of delicious cookies. And she posted on Facebook her thoughts and observations about staying the hell home. Every day. For 100 days.

She has now collected these observations in a book. A book you will love. Sheri's words will help you remember a time that you were certain you would never forget. But we're human. And we all do. Forget what we were certain at the time we would remember forever.

Sheri's words will make you smile, and laugh, and cry, and think, and feel. Sheri's words will help you feel more alive. And more "normal." And more connected. And most of all, I hope Sheri's words will help you feel grateful. More grateful. That people like my neighbor, now friend Sheri, exist in this world. Be like Sheri and gift this celebration of an ordinary extraordinary 100 days to someone—everyone—you love.

#lotsoflove,
Tom Zuba

Introduction

As the coronavirus pandemic worked its way into our country, states, counties, cities, and our homes, things began to change. *#understatementofthecentury*

I live in Illinois and our governor announced that the state would "Shelter-in-Place" effective Friday, March 13, 2020. For the next two weeks, only "essential" businesses and services would remain open.

Grocery stores became overwhelmed with people buying up all the toilet paper, disinfectant wipes, hand sanitizer, and chocolate. *#maybethatwasjustme*

Little did we know then that new words and phrases would seep into our daily vocabulary. Shelter-in-place, flatten the curve, quarantine, social distancing, wash your hands, stay-at-home, all in together, essential workers, masks, face coverings, and unprecedented times became common language. (If we all could have received a dollar for every time "unprecedented times" was uttered, the economy would be in great shape.)

My husband stepped into an Irish pub the night before bars and restaurants were ordered to close and even his pint of stout had our new mantra "Keep Calm and Wash Your Hands" designed in the foam. *#onemorebeforewego*

While no one could anticipate how long shelter-in-place would last, my thoughts were that it would be short term rather than long term, especially since our state order was initially only through end of March. I didn't panic. I went to Sherwin Williams and bought a couple gallons of paint so my husband could paint the dining room since we would be home with nothing better to do. I also set out to plan one family activity a night to keep us entertained. We dusted off the *Mayberryopoly* board game and played that on Saturday night. Sunday night we put new batteries in the controllers for Wii Bowling and had some fun competition. But our nightly fun fizzled out soon after it started. We just did like always, hanging out at the dinner table, discussing the weather, watching NetFlix, and chatting up on social media.

Shelter-in-place didn't fade away. Staying at home was the new normal. (Another phrase we adopted in 2020.) Me? Before I knew it, I was creating, and posting to Facebook, a daily Top 10 list of All Things COVID-19 that had creeped into my life. My posts mentioned whatever came to my mind. Some items and incidents were minor inconveniences, some were silver linings, some were comical; few were actual hardships. My nightly list was cathartic for me, and became highly popular with my friends, family, and followers on social media. So, I kept it up. Never could I have imagined that I would do it for 100 days. AND that this virus has not made its exit yet. *#stillunprecedentedtimes*

With a grateful heart, my family and I have remained healthy. And I have been asked to compile my list in book form. *#thanksoprah #wasntoprah*

My hashtags were appreciated, and I hope you find a chuckle or two here as well. I also hope this finds you safe and healthy, and in the mood for some levity. Grab a drink, wash your hands, and quarantine yourself. Settle in and get comfortable. We have 100 days to review of staying the hell home during COVID-19 2020.

The Warm-Up

March 13 – March 23, 2020

The first weekend of the shelter-in-place declaration took shape in a fast and furious way. It was the dress rehearsal to all that would be shut down in the extremely near future. *#stores #schools #prosports #broadway #lifeasweknewit*

I, like many people, had a vacation that was foiled due to coronavirus. My travel plans had been recreational in nature and in the big scheme really did not matter, yet cancelling my non-refundable, non-essential trip to New York City with my daughter was disappointing. I had taken out flight insurance for the airline tickets, but not the hotel. That wasn't very smart. The hotel charge was more than the airfare. *#liveandlearn*

Eventually, I received credit vouchers for the airlines and a refund on the hotel fee. We were hopeful that we could use those vouchers before the end of 2020. *#stillgrounded*

At home, throngs of people flocked to the grocery stores and cleared the shelves. My gig economy job as an independent contractor for a major grocery shopping service became extremely frustrating. Crowded aisles, naked shelves, no suitable substitutions for items, and the long lines to check out created a difficult work experience. I shouted it from the rooftops, (well, on Facebook), to select "use best judgement" as preferred method of communication with your shopper. The critical time lost with the back-and-forth conversations with the customer on out of stock items was detrimental in filling orders and accomplishing the vast number of orders that were placed. *#essentialworker #sheritheshiptshopper #exhausting #nevercouldhaveimagined #takewhatyoucanget*

The grocery stores soon implemented reduced hours and special early shopping hours for those most at risk of COVID-19. High touch points around the store were frequently sanitized or removed all together. No longer could you select your own donuts from the self-serve case or order salads from the deli. Adhesive arrows were applied to the floor and we followed traffic flow patterns up and down the aisles. Occasionally, someone would mutter or grumble something under his breath if I was going the wrong direction. *#haveagooddaybuddy*

While the grocery business was bustling in a highly unusual way, other stores and businesses had to close. Media outlets stressed the need to support local businesses. My family did. Our first take-out meal was chicken parmesan from a local restaurant that already had a thriving carry-out business, but they took it up a notch and set up a 2-lane drive, number system, payment station and parking. It went so smoothly. A few weeks later, another local restaurant was totally overwhelmed with take-out orders and not accustomed to managing this new way of doing business. It did not go so smoothly. *#chimichangas*

Curbside service became a new buzzword. One restaurant provided a roll of toilet paper in a party favor bag with each take-out order. *#ingenious #desperatetimes #desperatemeasures*

E-learning became a new way of life for many school kids and college students. Parents became teachers as school districts rushed to roll out some form of virtual learning/ remote classes as well as a system to provide students with technological devices and internet service at home. Our kitchen table quickly became a desk as we fired up an old laptop for a mass communication class that my son was taking at the community college. *#hugestruggle*

Originally, schools were shutting down for an extra week over Spring Break. No one could have predicted that students would not return. We naively assumed the stay-at-home order was for a couple weeks. We would ride this out and get back to "normal." Obviously, that did not happen. *#somekindofbadmovie*

How quickly we have become used to it all. Well, sort of. But back in the early days of the Shelter-in-Place order, this new way of doing things was different, unsettling, and just plain weird. *#newnormal*

The coronavirus was the boss. The pandemic created all kinds of changes in our lives. We all had to learn to do things differently. Flattening the curve to reduce the risk was going to be first attempted by staying home. And washing our hands. And social distancing. *#iwantanewboss*

Some habits we were able to keep. Like social media. And so, I posted. Here we go. *#100days*

Part One

Shelter-in-Place

March 22 – May 16, 2020

Day 1

March 22, 2020

It's Sunday.

Many businesses are closing, but my son is considered an essential worker—Matt works as a play companion at a children's long-term care facility—so he went in at his regularly scheduled time.

This is the only thing that was usual about our schedule today. *#stayhome #covid19*

Day 2

March 23, 2020

The things I accomplished today on the first business day of shelter-in-place:

1) I slept until 9 am. What, am I a teenager all over again?

   #ohgoodheavensno

2) My retirement job is working as an independent contractor for Shipt, a major on-line/on-demand shopping service. I normally shop six to eight grocery orders each day. I only shopped one today but bought a bag of Twizzlers and a head of cauliflower for myself. Magically, I only ate five pieces of licorice.

   #discipline

3) The community college announced it was going to host on-line courses instead of in-person classes. My son, Matt, needed help getting set up for the virtual learning and while scrolling through my cell phone for a specific app, I stumbled across my dear,

deceased dad's voice on the app. I had totally forgotten I had that on my phone.

#voicememo #app #totally rocks

4) In an ongoing project to ensure my insurance policies are up to date with appropriate beneficiaries, I continued to change that paperwork with the correct legal language for Matt's special needs trust.

#meetingwithlawyer #gratis

5) All throughout the day, I wondered how families with young kids at home are staying ahead of meal prep, dishes, and food in the house with everyone home.

#onlythreeofus #crazyenough
#gonnahidemylicorice

6) My professional career was spent in the field of special education as a teacher and supervisor. I worry about kids at homes where there is alcoholism, abuse, neglect, violence, other trauma and/or food insufficiency.

#pleasepray #followuponyourconcerns

7) This was my husband's first day where his office is closed, but a "work from home" system is not set up yet. I stayed out of his way as he worked on a home improvement project and I only offered compliments and encouragement.

#nohovering #wisewife

8) I changed the pillowcases on one pillow, but not the other two.

#thatisweird

9) I thought about changing all the sheets and pillowcases tomorrow, so the two pillowcases don't feel socially distanced from the rest of their squad in the laundry basket.

#newbuzzwords

10) Live theater has been a family favorite for us. We like youth performances, high school plays, community theater, Broadway, etc. Matt saves all the playbills, so I rounded up and recycled all the duplicates we had in the house. If anyone needs one from the last ten years or so from the Starlight community theater, I probably have it.

#breakaleg

I am not sure what is on my list for tomorrow, but I'm not bored yet.

Day 3

Amusing myself on Day 3 of shelter-in-place:

1) Did you know that shredding paper takes two machines? One to shred the paper and one to vacuum up the mess.

   #scrapseverywhere

2) I enjoy decorating my mailbox with seasonal covers. One big accomplishment today was taking down with the winter cardinal cover and putting up the Easter one, just so the folks passing by know I am aware of the current season.

   #changewiththetimes

3) The bottom drawer in the kitchen is a secret hide-out drawer. The Valentine M&M's taste just as good after St. Patrick's Day as they did before then.

   #pinkisthenewgreen

4) We well-endowed women have struggles. The "girl" on the left always proves who's

boss to the "girl" on the right and it is most noticeable in bright-colored t-shirts!

#lopsided #unevenbrastraps #shouldiwearblack

5) Some people love coffee, but I love McDonald's Diet Coke. The plastic lids are embossed with whimsical quips that say things like "Drinking of You" and "Feeling Bubbly."

#cheapthrills #stilladollar

6) Since we're stuck at home, I thought I should show something for my time. I took out the Murphy's Oil Soap and filled a bucket with water. Smell is such a powerful memory trigger. I remembered Esther, who supervised us while cleaning the religious order's house at my high school during the summer.

#workingofftuition #longtimeago

7) Craig, a beloved neighbor, often cooked, baked, and shared some tasty recipes. There is such sentimental value having a recipe with his handwriting on it. Tonight's dinner was his recipe for barley vegetable soup.

#delicious #goodmemories #thankscraig

8) My husband and Matt are members of a local Lions of Illinois chapter. The widow of a former member gave Matt her husband's Lion signature jacket. It fit Matt perfectly. If we had not been sheltered-in-place, I would not have been home to admire him wearing

this special jacket as he returned from his daily walk.

#lionsclub #fellowship #snazzyjacket

9) Church Picture Directories: I was leafing through the pages of the 2013 directory during dinner to see if there would be someone who might appreciate some of the soup I had made.

#peoplehavechanged #needanewdirectory

#souptoospicyanyway

10) *Toy Story* is one of our family's favorite movies of all time. We had a cherished juice glass with Buzz and Woody on it that probably came with jelly in it or something. It broke today.

#bummer #toinfinityandbeyond

Day 4

March 25, 2020

Wins for today!

1) The geraniums are going crazy!

   #winteredinside

2) It is possible to scrape one-year old paint off the bottom of a scrub bucket.

   #whoknew?

3) *Per stirpes*: A phrase I learned as I went about my business of updating records. The Catholic Mass is not the only place where I have learned some words in Latin.

   #perstirpes #meansgrandkids

4) I dissuaded my husband from running to Taco Bell with a partially used gift card with a day-old sandwich from the grocery store instead.

   #lunchathome #thriftywife

5) The governor started a daily press conference on the coronavirus update. Since it was 4:00

in the afternoon, we felt it should be paired with a cocktail.

#fiveoclocksomewhere

6) I packaged up an overdue birthday present for my great niece along with a little something special for my sister.

#travelingphantomgift
#countrychurchdecoration #familyfun

7) Vacuuming is therapeutic, except when there is too much cleaning up to do before you get started. Then it is not therapeutic. I pulled a pillow out from behind my son's bed and organized his yearbooks. I decluttered by putting some other things in the recycle bin. Then it was time to make dinner.

#neverturnediton

8) I realized that sleeping until 7 or 7:30 am, or later, could become habit-forming with no place to go and nothing to do.

#shelterinplace #stayhome #sleepmore

9) While finishing a couple of grocery orders today, I had never noticed how fun it is to sit in my car in the parking lot and watch other people load their groceries.

#whohasbigdogs #whodrinkssoda #whowhistles

10) I read an article that was in the Chicago Tribune that totally moved me. How people

survive loss, grieve, find hope, and love again always amazes me.

#lovewins

Day 5

March 26, 2020

Things that make "stay-at-home" so worthwhile:

1) Staying up late because the next day's schedule is loose. Daylight savings time is an adjustment.

   #noplacetogo

2) Time to read the daily papers in one sitting. Well, one is the local paper and only has two skimpy sections now. We get two daily papers delivered.

   #oldschool #keepingpeopleemployed #newspapercarrier

3) Being caught off guard and taking a moment to pause and honor a short, six car (including the hearse) funeral procession, traveling to a cemetery. During this time of quarantine, people are grieving alone.

   #devastating

4) Two more desk drawers are now empty because of all the purging and shredding going on.

   #somejobsfinallygettingdone

5) Stepping back into my teacher mode to explain how to play Yahtzee.

   #create #visualaid

6) Pouring a rum and Coke in a tall glass and fondly recalling the good times with old friends from my early teaching years.

   #cheers

7) Cooking with Matt and preparing a recipe from a VIP breakfast he has worked in the past. Thanks to whoever "invented" pre-cooked bacon and sausage crumbles!

   #shortcuts #sanity

8) Really giving some thought to going paper-less on my last "holdout" accounts.

   #hateonlinepasswords

9) Considering putting the container of Clorox wipes I found under the sink tonight up for bid to see how much I could get for it.

   #prettydarnvaluable

10) No mail from Social Security in about two days! Presuming they put the people in the office on a work-at-home schedule. Whoop! Whoop!

    #winwin

We all need to stay home. We need to kick this virus in the rear.

Day 6

March 27, 2020

Subtle ways that the coronavirus affected us today:

1) Doctor appointment: Matt's office appointment was changed to an over-the-phone appointment. My husband said Matt did splendidly by answering the doctor's questions, reporting his blood pressure and temperature.

   #adultingagain

2) Schedules: My husband's work-at-home day turned into a vacation day. I am not a fan.

   #stayatyourdesk

3) Hold times: I am still completing paperwork and dread hearing "we are experiencing a high volume of phone calls and your wait time could be longer than usual." Then the next recorded message is "your wait time will be less than 1 minute."

   #quickie

4) New York City: This would have been my last day in New York City with my daughter on her last spring break trip.

#savingourcoldhardcash

5) Facebook Flash Sale: On a very unprecedented move, I had ordered some walking shoes for my NYC trip. The information said there could be a delay in shipping due to volume. No big deal, right? Then I noticed there was a $1.13 international debit fee charged to my account. Yes, the shoes are coming from China.

#disinfect #thirtysevendollarsinthehole

6) Jellybeans: I had bought several bags that were meant to be divided for small appreciation packages for the grocery store workers where I shop for Shipt, but with all the concern over the virus, the jellybeans have become a secret stash here at home. They are almost gone.

#sendreinforcements

7) Fish Fry Friday: We would have gone out to a fish fry tonight because it's Lent, but instead we warmed up eggplant parmesan from Pinnon's, a delightful local corner meat store, and baked some shrimp instead. I used the shiny new pan my mother-in-law gave me for Christmas. It makes me feel like a newlywed all over again! No, not that kind of

newlywed! You know, the new kitchen stuff kind of newlywed.

#whatwereyouthinking

8) Weird schedule: Every day is unscheduled now. I have too many deep-dive projects going on and I cannot get back to the book I started reading. I'm stuck in the middle of *Where the Crawdads Sing* and I can't get going again.

#readtwentyminutes #everyday #thirdgrademantra

9) Newspaper article: There was a local online story today about grocery delivery being an essential service. Our orders have grown exponentially.

#lovemycoworkers #mostofthemanyway

10) Take time to play: I noticed some croquet racks set up in a yard when I delivered a grocery order. One of the silver linings in the pandemic is for kids and adults to do something together.

#powerdowndevices

Day 7

March 28, 2020

Shelter-in-Place: Literally

It is very reassuring to have so many friends point out on Facebook that there is a tornado warning for our area. Like, perhaps, I wouldn't obviously know why the tornado sirens were blaring?

1) We just emerged from the basement. That tornado warning brought new meaning to shelter-in-place.

   #markedsafe

2) There is a surprise in every box! Remember the days of a free prize in cereal boxes and Cracker Jack? The grocery stockers filled the toilet paper aisle with cereal last night. The produce guy said maybe people would think there would be a surprise in the bottom of the box, and it would be a roll of toilet paper!

   #dontsqueezethecharmin

3) The toilet paper shortage/hoarding is insane, but the funny memes going around Facebook are hilarious.

   #giggles

4) With all this at-home time, it's fun to try new drinks or visit an old favorite. A friend served herself a Captain Morgan and Coke, after not having drank soda for a year, because she saw a picture posted on Facebook.

   #caved #unprecedentedtimes #picturesarepersuasion

5) The whimsical quip on the lid of my favorite soft drink today made me smile. Sorry for Starbucks' lovers. Make the switch . . . McDonald's is still open!

   #sipforjoy #drivethrough

6) No limes! Two of my orders wanted limes today. Neither the grocery store nor Target had them. One was for guacamole and one was for margaritas. No Patron tequila, substitute with 1800 Silver Tequila and concentrated lime juice.

   #improvise

7) The local paper runs a weekend supplement called the "Go" section. I joked that it could have been skipped this week because everything is either cancelled or closed. The premier of the movie filmed here in town (*Without Grace*) has now been rescheduled for August 1, 2020.

   #sonisanextra #metoo #moviestars

8) Hand sanitizer: The local distilleries are switching over to making hand sanitizer.

   #clever

9) Lacking resources: I still worry about the families that do not have appropriate things in their homes for kids to do or enough good food to eat. The schools and community programs are providing sack lunches as well as other outreach efforts by churches, etc. Are we reaching everyone?

#keeppraying #dowhateveryoucan

10) Stay home. Shelter-in-place. Flatten the curve.

#homesweethome

Day 8

March 29, 2020

Sunday—Long Day

1) The day started out well. Jeannie C. Riley was singing "Harper Valley PTA" on the country oldies station. I imagine there will be some creative parodies or ballads in time to humor us. Something like "Social Distance Valley My Oh My!"

   #singit

2) Cloth face masks: A lady was wearing one in the store today that said F***off. Now, was that necessary?

   #idontthinkso

3) Mass: My husband observed Mass from our church via live stream and Matt watched one that was being live streamed in another city. Maybe next week we will observe Mass at the Basilica of the National Shrine of the Immaculate Conception in Washington, DC.

   #beenthere

4) Nothing like making me crazy when I can't figure out something in the first twenty min-

utes. I am grateful that my husband is here to rescue us when I give up on trying to help get my son's technology situated for his virtual classes. E-learning is not for the easily frustrated!

#makesmecrabby

5) The cupboards are not bare by any standard in this house, but it is time to pop the kettle corn dated "Best used by Oct 2018."

#poppedjustfine

6) I am trying to read further in my library book. I think there were a few snoozes in between some of the pages.

#letsgettothegoodpart

7) Everyone's jumping on the Zoom app and connecting with their people. My son's camp crowd had some fun with that today, too.

#cooltechnology

8) The newspaper ran the printed article on grocery delivery service today: "Shopping for Others in Pandemic Times." Many shoppers worked their booties off this weekend. I stayed home for the most part.

#storesarecrazy

9) There are now new guidelines for putting out the garbage. There are so many essential workers to whom I have not given too much thought.

#alljobsarenecessary

10) It has been a long day. There is not a number ten unless you want to know how many blouses, tops, and sweaters are in my sisters' and sister-in-law's closets. They have been purging.

#clothingdonations

On to a new week. Stay well!

Day 9 or 10

March 30, 2020

Day 9 or 10 of Shelter-in-Place?

1) The newspaper ran a gallery of pictures illustrating what our city looks like during this pandemic and the "Stay-at-Home" order. The article said yesterday was Day 9, so I will go with that. If you are keeping track, today is Day 10 and there are so many more days to come.

2) False hope: When I woke up today, I saw orange and yellow vehicle lights blinking outside my bedroom window. For a second, I thought it was a school bus and then I remembered school is out.

   #darn #itwasagarbagetruck

3) Produce mark-downs: It was surprising to see that some items were marked down at the store today. I thought maybe that the panic had subsided, and folks were not clamoring for groceries like they have been the past two weeks. Not apparently so. There are still so many bare shelves and it is kind of frustrating to work some orders. The secret

is out though, eggs come in on Mondays and Thursdays. I am like the town crier and ask my customers if they want a second dozen if they have eggs on their order.

#limittwodozen

4) Blood drive: I was shocked to see a mobile blood unit parked at McDonald's today. We know there is always a need. I messaged my husband to tell him as I thought he would consider it as an excuse to get out of the house. He gives red cells and did not think they would be doing that in a mobile unit. Silly him, I think he missed an opportunity to take this as a chance to get out of the house and at least ask them.

#stayedathome

5) Slippery slope: We're not living in a precise world right now, so it is not the time to figure it down to the penny. When you tip, it is cool to round up or round down. $6.08 is an unusual tip on a grocery order, even if it was 10%. On another note, it seemed today at least, that the number of orders for groceries has subsided a bit. Are we in a breathing space until everyone's stash has dwindled, and we will start all over again with the frenzy?

#toiletpaper #shortage

6) My great niece loves the Disney movie, *Frozen*, like all kids probably do. Today she received the package I sent her. My sister is awesome about doing interactive things with her and

they made the cake balls from the *Frozen* kit. Since we are home, let's all spend our time wisely. Show kids the things you know.

#teachingmoments #learningopportunities

7) A few years ago, I got a little wooden country church decoration in a silent auction basket. The small church now secretly travels from home to home in my extended family. You never know when it is going to pop up in an inconspicuous place in your house after we have all been together. I am at a disadvantage because they live near each other and it gets passed around more frequently. I have had it for a long time, but now one of my sisters is the new church lady, compliments of adding it to my niece's birthday package.

#surprise #churchshelterinplace

8) Neighborhood Walkers: There are three big windows in the front room of my house. It is a great place to watch people walk by—or join them, while social distancing, of course.

#getwalking #dontgainquarantine15

9) Pinnon's has the best meats, homemade frozen dinners, and do not even get me started on their Rice Krispie treats! Give yourself a meal planning break and head over there for something different.

#shoplocal

10) Some nights get quite late when I finish and upload my Top 10 list. I see comments

posted on the previous day's post that folks are looking for the new one, so I know it's time to "hurry up already." I can tell when my sister is waiting on her end for the new post. Sit back, relax, we will all be around for a few more days.

#nightowls

Day 10

March 31, 2020

Quality of Life: Shelter-in-Place

1) I stayed up very late to finally finish my book. It was so good, but took me a really long time to read. And FYI, I am not going to "*Where the Crawdads Sing.*"

#spooky

2) As I parked my car in the Target parking lot, I was excited to see the girl in the car next to me was reading. Bummer! She was not reading.

#onherphone

3) "Ahh, So Tasty" was the whimsical quip on the lid of my Diet Coke today and put some pep in my step.

#giddyup

4) A customer gave another shopper and me some cucumber melon scented hand sanitizer yesterday. Another one gave me some apple scented sanitizer a while ago. It's nice to have them show us their concern.

#washyourhands #sanitizer #inapinch

5) I exercised today. I hopped down a hopscotch drawn in chalk on a driveway during one of my deliveries.

#needasportsbra

6) I am still learning new legal terms. A Medallion Signature Guarantee is something that you must get at the bank. Since the bank lobbies are closed, I need to schedule an appointment with a banker and send my paperwork through the drive-through tube for the signature.

#notnotarypublic #unprecedentedtimes #canigetasuckertoo

7) I asked my husband to go to CVS with coupons for Easter cards and vitamins. He got the vitamins but not the Easter cards. Oops. And he went to Walgreens instead of CVS.

#cvsoupons #cvscouponsdontworkatwalgreens

8) The ginger beer I found hidden in the crisper drawer of the refrigerator was probably going to expire/exceed "best used by" date since it was in there for a while (11/2019). I am not afraid of too many expired dates.

#wellmaybe #ifitslambchops

9) I have decided I am finished with diffusers and candle warmers with those little wax cubes. I had both of my diffusers going in the same room today. I could not smell any lovely smells.

#needbetteroils #goodwilldonation

10) As I was preparing a real dinner for a change, I got distracted looking in the pantry and cupboards for the poppy seeds. But I found I still have a jar of Juniper berries for a recipe I made a long time ago. I only needed five or six of them to make elk that my cousin in Alaska sent us a few years ago.

#mysonfindsthedarndestrecipes

11) We pretended to have a dinner party tonight and ate in the newly painted dining room. We even broke out the Easter napkins.

#plasticeggsarenext

12) I just wondered if you are still reading and noticed that I went over my limit of Top 10.

#whoiscounting

Day 11

April 1, 2020

Things that made me go "huh?":

1) The long line of cars that stretched from a local high school to a local church early this morning (about 0.5 mile).

   #notafuneral #chromebooks #distribution #elearning

2) I noticed too late that I dripped make-up on my work t-shirt, again!

   #selfconscious #allday #essentialworker

3) I wondered why the Q-tip company makes a package of 625 count, but they are not stocked on the shelf with the other ones. Who thinks of these crazy quantities? What is wrong with the standard 375, 500 or 750 count packages?

   #scavengerhunt #professionalshopperstruggles

4) DIY hand sanitizer: I learned that two parts of aloe vera gel to one part of 91% rubbing alcohol makes a do-it-yourself hand sanitizer. But rubbing alcohol is sold out, too!

   #washyourhands #againandagain

5) "Jump for Joy" was the quip on my pop lid today. Obviously, McDonald's does not know me very well. Jumping for joy without a good supportive undergarment is disastrous.

#girlsgirlsgirls #whereismy18hourbra

6) On a rare occasion, I get lunch from a fast-food drive-through restaurant. There is that moment when you reach in the bag for that last French fry and you get the paper from your straw.

#surprise #doesnttastelikechicken

7) It was a beautiful spring day here in the Midwest. A lovely woman at the grocery store sat in a lawn chair in the parking lot and enjoyed the sunshine while her friend went in for the groceries. Now that is how you go to the store together!

#socialdistancing #noneedfor2toshop

8) Purging obsolete records: I was begrudgingly reminded that my son's payback for an over payment from Social Security will continue until June 2024. I bet that they will change that many more times before then!

#interestfree #stillmakesmenuts

9) Dinner from Pinnon's: meatloaf and cheesy potatoes. That meal was supposed to be for my husband and son when I was in New York City.

#darncovid #istillheartNY

10) For once there was an e-learning assignment that I could help Matt with for his Audio Recording class. I helped him prepare an outline for the Public Service Announcement. I love a little creative writing time.

#classof77 #yearbookeditor

Day 12

April 2, 2020

Feeling melancholy.

I feel like I am living in someone else's country, on the other side of the world. Our rules of society have changed so much. So much of what we do is so different. I am not feeling lonely while sheltering-in-place but noticing the things I am doing differently or what the people around me are doing differently.

1) My husband is working at home. Simultaneously, he is working on the pool by starting to fill it with water to detect the precise location of the leak. He usually doesn't start pool work this early in the season.

   #waterisrunning #continuously

2) People in the grocery stores are wearing masks and gloves. This is not normal. I feel like we are in a terrorist country. I guess the coronavirus is the terrorist.

   #covid19

3) The long line of traffic today for emergency support was for diapers and formula. A local church realized and witnessed a critical need.

   #thankyou

4) The weather has gotten nice and the parks and playgrounds beckon. But the park district had to remove basketball hoops, backboards, and soccer nets to discourage groups from congregating.

#stayathome #itshard

5) I am doing things I usually dislike because I now have the time. I unraveled the phone charger that got sucked up in the beater bar of the vacuum cleaner when Matt vacuumed his room today. That kind of stuff is usually my husband's job.

#tada #ididit

6) School is so different for kids. I have seen some fun things teachers are doing with distance learning and seeing how many of my friends are approaching it with humor with their kids. I have a friend who has a very heartbreaking and complicated family story. If there is ever one to carry on, it is this guy. He is doing some e-learning with his two daughters who have various disabilities and challenges. Two of his lessons today from "Jim's Institute" were Charcuterie Class and Tech Ed for Young Ladies. They prepared a cold-cut lunch and carried a few pickets for a fence repair. I love this guy. His humor tickles me down deep. He keeps going. He stays the course. We must, too.

#momdad #cancersucks #patioIEPhangoutmeeting

7) My pop lid today was uneventful. But I drank the soda anyway.

#thatwasgood

8) The city's new garbage pick-up protocol is that everything must be in a bin or container. I asked my 89-year-old retired History teacher/customer today if she would like me to bring her corrugated cardboard back to the garage, since it wasn't picked up. I noticed she had secured it with strips of cloth. That was her generation—repurpose everything. Now I feel like we are conserving and rationing everything.

#reduce #reuse #recycle

9) Radio stations are interrupted with coronavirus updates. We are used to the Tuesday morning emergency broadcast alerts and now we are getting used to the virus updates, too. That emergency alert the other day calling for the return of retired health care workers was unnerving.

#yikes #sad #scary

10) Someone on a Facebook page I follow mentioned his stimulus check was already deposited in his account. That seemed surprisingly fast to me.

#lostjobs #lostbusiness #etc

I feel like I am Charlie Brown or Eeyore today. Woe is me. I should be back to my Peppermint Patty self tomorrow.

Day 13

April 3, 2020

Enter Refresh Mode:

If you have been following along, you may want to sit back, relax, and come along for the ride. There is a lot to say today.

1) Masks: A good friend had some N95 masks and gave me one. She also gave me a "Putting on a Mask: 101" lesson—they are trickier than you think. Besides the obvious precautions of why we wear masks now, there's added benefits: no need to apply lipstick throughout the day, mouth breathing is more effective than nasal breathing, vanity goes out the window, bobby pins are useful since your ears now keep the mask in place but there's no space for your hair. On the flip side, there's disadvantages: they're hot, they're hard to keep clean, you can smell your breath in them, and they unfortunately whisk a diamond earring out of your ear when you take it off. She retraced her steps in the grocery store parking lot and she found it!

   #faith #praytostanthony

2) Soap: Bath and Body Works foam soap is so much better than the grocery store brand foam soap.

#keepwashing #christmassoapinapril

3) Cancellations: There's so much disappointment. Weddings, proms, graduations, showers, birthday parties, sleepovers, concerts, trips, lessons, dates, moves, and on and on, are cancelled and postponed. We had hoped to see the Nielsen Trust (Cheap Trick's Rick Nielsen, Miles Nielsen, and Kelly Steward) concert last night, but it is rescheduled for December.

#cheaptrick #originalrockfordband

4) Radio: It takes a village to stop a virus. That is exactly what the radio announcer said.

#stayhome #flattenthecurve

5) Mother-in-law and brother-in-law: My mother-in-law will be 93 this month. My brother-in-law has been the sole reason she has been able to stay at home and we are ever so grateful. They have committed to this arrangement and as you may know, caregiving over the long haul is tough. My husband checks in each day and is willing to help, but now it is even more difficult to provide that support.

#minimizecontactwithothers #distancelove

6) Enter Refresh Mode: McDonald's got it right today. I needed to refresh my attitude. A

contactless effort was made for the payment transaction when the cashier slid an empty plastic box out through the drive-through window for me to place my money. It was kind of like a collection basket at church. I thought I would have to kiss my twenty-dollar bill goodbye though because the wind was blowing and there wasn't anything to hold it down. At least they could have placed a Big Mac on the bill as a paperweight!

#innovative

7) Fish Fry: The bottom-line is don't do it at home! Order out! We tried, we failed. Let the experts handle it!

#misscatholicchurchfishfrys #Lent #carryout

8) Oops! I retrieved a candle from the closet to absorb the fish smell and thump! The whole box of candles slipped off the closet shelf and shattered everywhere. My husband chose to clean up that disaster over the kitchen mess.

#needmorecandlesnow

9) Ellen: Life is fragile. A friend's daughter died last night. Ellen was in 8th grade and experienced a sudden cerebral incident. We are heartbroken for the family. During this time of quarantine and isolation, I cannot imagine how much more pain this causes. What I do know is that there are ways to support people during their time of tragedy and grief. My well-respected good friend and author, Tom Zuba, has shared many things we can do to be present in these moments:

1. Say the name of the person who died. Not just today, but tomorrow, next week, later this month, next month, three months from now, on their birthday, during the holidays, etc. You get the idea.

2. Cry with the grieving person, cry for them, sit with them while they cry. Don't stop the tears—yours or theirs.

3. Write a personal note. Share stories, memories, and pictures.

4. In time, ask them how they are doing and allow them to tell you how they are doing/feeling. It may be raw, but it is necessary. The tears may fall again and that will be ok. There are so many more ways to support someone in their grief. During this pandemic, more than ever, reach out to your friends and family who might be very vulnerable for so many reasons.

#permissiontomourn #tomzuba #amazon

10) Here we are. We are two weeks into shelter-in-place. We cannot get lazy or take short-cuts. We need to stay the course. We've got this.

#thisisus

Day 14

April 4, 2020

Just another day in paradise:

1) DIY Masks: The Do-It-Yourself masks are coming out in all shapes, sizes, and colors. The most improvised ones were the guy wearing a terry cloth hand towel that was jimmy-rigged across his face and another guy with a paper towel folded in some origami manner and secured with some kind of elastic. I swear, the people who are wearing kerchiefs in bandit fashion are out to play "cops and robbers."

   #truth #DIYcreativity

2) Gloves: My improved COVID-19 fashion appearance included the real use of a bobby pin and a pair of gloves a co-worker gave me. I totally felt like a burglar with my black gloves.

   #macburglar #newkindofday

3) Smiles: Once your mouth is covered by a mask, how can someone tell if you are smiling or if you have your crabby face on? Well, I told the grocery stocker that I was smiling

as I said good morning. He told me he could see the rise in my cheekbones, so he knew I was smiling.

#keepsmiling #saycheese

4) TWICE! Twice I have asked my husband to go to CVS to get Easter cards with my coupons. I thought he would like a reason to get out of the house. He went to the right store today but left the darn coupons at home. I even set them next to his wallet before he left! So there goes 30% off regular priced merchandise and $1.99 off three cards. I'll have to tell my mom to enjoy the Easter card twice as much because it was full price!

#twice #youhadonejob #endrant

5) Lazy days: It is getting pretty darn easy to sleep in. Grocery orders roll out in the early morning and the on-demand service has exploded since the virus disrupted our lives. Since there are plenty of orders all day and evening there is no need to hang an arm out of bed to silence the phone at 6:02 a.m.

#noalarm #sleepisgood #lastoneup #makesthebed

6) McDonald's: Nothing to report here.

#movealong

7) Frozen pizza and social distancing: For the love of God, we do not need the mom and teenage son staring at the empty frozen pizza cases. Pick a frozen Jack's cheese pizza or Red Barron crispy crust pepperoni and move

the heck along. The Tombstones are out of stock, for gosh sake. Better yet, leave the kid at home.

#onepersonpickspizza #clustersofpeople #covid19violation #shopalone

8) Caramel corn: I asked Matt to think about something he would like to do or make for a together-at-home activity. He picked movie night, so we watched *On the Wings of a Dove* with Alex Jennings (1998). I decided to pull out an incredibly old caramel corn recipe that I have probably only made once since I got it in the 1980's. Let's say it was more successful than our fish fry.

#bakenotfry #moviesnack

9) Lunch: Breakfast and dinner are easy, but "What's for lunch?" is by far the biggest challenge of the day. You would think there would be groceries in the house for all the time I spend in the grocery store.

#fendforthemselves #havesomecereal

10) Help wanted: We need help getting the software programs and apps downloaded to help Matt set up the computer for his audited class.

#elearning #stillstruggling #needcollegelab

Tomorrow is Sunday. I may "go" to church in Washington, DC. *#masstimes.org #livestream*

Day 15

April 5, 2020

Things that made Sunday a shelter-in-place Sunday:

1) Church at home is just not the same, even though my son embraces the whole experience. He kneels, prays, and sings. We all prayed the "Our Father" out loud, but I think I missed some of the sermon.

   #nap

2) The realization that your pork butt shoulder is too big for your crock pot makes you shake your darn head. Also, why does one piece of meat have two body part names?

   #buttshoulder #roasterpans #veryhelpful

3) The tarragon vinegar bottle has a sealed wrapper on it as if it were a bottle of wine. It will probably expire before I ever use it again.

   #icook #hedoeslaundry

4) Things are getting serious with personal protective equipment (PPE). A guy in the grocery store today had on a mask, gloves, and a hazmat suit. Masks (and crayon drawings)

were left out for me at one delivery. Another little four-year-old friend drew a picture of a grocery bag, complete with handles. At another place, two cute redheads came out to help unload, as they always do, but wearing masks today.

#facecoverings #besafe

5) I think I heard a quick news headline state that there weren't any new cases reported in our county today.

#arelabsclosed #flattenthecurve

6) McDonald's: Jump for Joy. I did not. I got my Diet Coke on my way back from one delivery and headed to the store for the next order. No way can I sip a soda in the store while wearing a mask.

#oops #badtimingformysoda

7) There was a bottle of Hiram Walker's Cream De Cacao in the cupboard for who knows how long.

#brandyalexanderstonight.

8) I sat for three uncharacteristic hours watching "The Academy of Country Music Presents: Our Country" followed by "Garth and Trisha Live in Studio G." My husband watched too, but it is doubtful he enjoyed either show too much.

#goodsport

9) My friend whose daughter died, and her family, are heavy on my heart tonight.

   #heartbroken

10) Easter is one week away. I know it is about more than just the baskets and candy, but it is not a good idea to wait till Thursday or Friday to get your favorites.

    #sourpatch #jellybeans #soldout
    #ewwww #brachsjellybeans #please

11) TurboTax is in the house.

    #onestep #atatime

Have a good week. Cover up. We will get through this.

Day 16

April 6, 2020

This and that:

1) It has been great to read all the comments on these posts. I appreciate that you're finding a time in your day to see what ordinary things are happening in my day while we all shelter-in-place. Today's edition is tomorrow's morning paper for some of you!

   #specialdelivery

2) I saw a sign today repeating the popular motto DON'T SWEAT THE SMALL STUFF. A long time ago, in 1996 and 1997, my husband and I learned quickly how to not sweat the small stuff. Our perspective changed drastically and immediately. It is much easier to pay attention to simple joys and ordinary experiences than to get in a tizzy over other things. Normal, everyday, amazing appreciations are everywhere. Always. Look for them.

   #sonsbraintumoratage2
   #learnthingsthehardway #silverlinings

3) Easter cards, in case you are wondering, went out in the mail today.

#postalservice #dontletmedown

4) Grocery delivery: Everything was good and well, including the thank you note that was taped to the door for me . . . until . . . I backed out of the driveway and knocked over a trash can and bag of sticks. I jumped out and up righted them, then continued to back out . . . and did it AGAIN! Two neighbors out working in their yards saw this happen both times. I would guess the lady of the house and her daughter were peeking out from their curtain and snickering, too!

#dontsweatit #shakingmyhead #gooddriveraward

5) Snacks: Honestly, without going on an all-out "eat healthy" program, I really do like sugar snap peas and raw cauliflower for a morning snack. Lawry's Seasoned Salt is amazing on the cauliflower.

#yum #easy #sugarsnappeasandIdontcare

6) For my friends who have or will have special needs trusts: I am still plugging away to get the beneficiaries situated on various things. One company cannot get past the fact that the trust does not have a tax ID number or Social Security number attached to it at this point. All the other companies did not have a problem with it. The lawyer gave me a workaround for it.

#timeconsuming #sheesh #canigetabreak

7) McDonald's: It was a two-soda day today. The first lid was "Feeling Bubbly" and why, yes, I was feeling bubbly with that one. Then, after a particularly large order in the afternoon, I felt the need to "Enter Refresh Mode."

#repeats #ohwell

8) Joy: I have many friends who are grounded. Not the stay-at-home kind of grounded, but the kind who do the right thing when no one is looking, who hold true to their morals and live them, who celebrate everyday joys, who struggle but hang on tight during the tough moments, and spread joy wherever they go. Elisa is that kind of person. She lets me know how much she appreciates me and sent a flower-balloon yard display today.

#surprise #beautiful #fun #groovy

9) Gloves: Some things really do get me in a tizzy (like those unused CVS coupons I mentioned the other day). Today it was another occasion where someone threw away their disposable gloves in the parking lot after grocery shopping. I was so ticked. I said to the guy who parked next to me: "Look at this! Look what someone did again!" He was as disgusted as I was, and he said it best: "On top of everything else going on!" That does not sound so profound now, but it sure fit the moment at the time.

#litterbug #disrespect #covid19

10) Jim's Institute: My funny friend who is the mom and dad in his family aligned his e-learning with their district's spring break. However, today he implemented an emergency home economics lesson because they were running critically low on cookies as well as chocolate chips. His daughter found some mini packs of M&Ms leftover from Halloween to make up the difference. They are my kind of people.

#makecookies #scrounge #lifeskills

11) Cold feet in bed: Corn bags are the best solution! Two minutes and 30 seconds in the microwave before you go to bed and I assure you your feet will be warm before you fall asleep.

#winterchill #springthaw

12) Today was Monday. The lawyer said he knew yesterday was Sunday because the "funnies" were in color. Yes, he is old and a little bit old school. But it is true. It is kind of hard to remember what day it is.

#shelterinplace #samestuff #differentday

So, there is a #12 tonight. It will be OK. Don't sweat the small stuff.

Day 17

A productive/constructive day:

1) A while ago the newspaper ran an article titled "100 Things to Do While Shelter-in-Place." One suggestion was to clean out your make-up drawer and get rid of old stuff. So, that is what I did. I started by using a Q-tip to clean the dust out of the drawer slide, then vacuumed the drawer, replaced the shelf liner and as the story goes, "*When You Give a Mouse a Cookie*" the rest is history.

   #mydrawersareclean

2) The jellybeans got spilled the other day. My son cleaned them up but as I was getting the vacuum, I spotted a yellow one on the floor. The 5-second rule can be a 5-day rule when it comes to jellybeans on the floor at our house. We are overachievers.

   #ateitrightup

3) These are unprecedented times. Case in point: I may throw something away that still works. My $2.00 garage sale hair dryer is

very old and has a loose cap. I am tired of it. Out it goes.

#cantbelieveitmyself

4) We are running critically low on jellybeans. Well, to be truthful, I am running low. I will add them to the list when my husband goes to the store to get marshmallow bunnies and marshmallow eggs for their Easter baskets. It doesn't matter to me if he goes to Walgreens or CVS. Marshmallow bunnies are not my thing. At all.

#nocoupons #passthejellybeans #butnottheblackones

5) The Smokin' Coop, a popular outdoor bar-beque restaurant is open for the season. This is worth mentioning as a public service announcement for my local friends.

#washyourhands #bbq

6) Dinner was Plan C tonight. There was something missing for anything I was going to make. And then I saw the Ramen noodles. I could ask "Who uses Ramen noodles?" but as evidenced at the grocery store, everyone does but me! They have been out of stock for days. I felt guilty and greedy having any in my pantry at all. I make that oriental cole-slaw recipe about once every two years with a package of Ramen. Yeah, that is probably another thing that is expired in my pantry.

#bestusdedbydates #meaningless #sometimes

7)   When "It's a Great Day to Be Alive" comes
      on the radio, I look to the heavens and
      rejoice. This song makes me smile and sing
      out loud every single time I hear it! Especially
      when the windows are down and the sun's
      shining in the neighborhood.

      #childrensoncologycamp
      #sobwhenihearthekidssing #lastingmemories

8)   My mom has an apartment in a senior living
      center. My brother and sister moved her to
      a corner apartment with a patio. Yep, it's a
      great day to be alive!

      #freshair

9)   I needed a little decompression time after an
      exceptionally large and complicated grocery
      order today. Thought I was being sneaky
      by putting my feet up for a bit when I got
      home but BUSTED! An on-line friend posted
      a status asking what our view was at that
      moment. Honest, I don't always wear black
      socks and shorts, but when I do, I am very
      comfy.

      #nojudgmentzone

10)   Dinner table conversations can be heavy
      sometimes. Like "maybe someone doesn't
      know they're grieving when they really are"
      as spoken by one who has so much more
      depth than I sometimes realize.

      #myson

11) The kitchen sink is full of dinner dishes. The Dawn dish soap is almost gone, and the store shelves are empty. It might be time to start ordering out to avoid having dishes, but let's hurry up and do it! Good Friday is coming.

#fasting #stomachwillbegrowling

Our first two-week period of shelter-in-place is over. That was the honeymoon. Now we are in for the grind. Stay the course. We've got this.

Day 18

April 8, 2020

Sights and sounds:

1) Overdue housekeeping at 7 am: When the urge strikes to wash the crisper drawers, I go with it. Many times, there's things hidden in there I have long forgotten.

   #pantryrefrigerator #gingerbeer #sproutedpotatoes #boyscoutpopcorn

2) Masks: After three or four days of wearing my N95 mask, it finally had to go. It kept slipping off my nose and probably was not all that effective anymore, anyway. But it had to have been far more effective than the woman in the store wearing a hospital isolation mask over her mouth but under her nose. Good grief, all the while talking way too loudly by the bacon to her husband that was over by the beef stew meat waving his cane towards the chicken case.

   #lordy #wearitright #ornotatall #andpipedown

3) Easter traditions: I cannot figure out why so many grocery orders have Rice Krispies and

marshmallows on them this week. Is that an Easter tradition?

#notforme #ricekrispietreats #bakesales

4) McDonald's: There's something new at the drive-through window. Plexiglass! The shield has yellow tape framing a large square in the middle. I did not know at first if it was a target and I was supposed to throw my money through it or what. Just kidding! When I realized it was a protective device, I asked the gal if I could take her picture and post it. You would have thought I had sent her to the moon and back!

#lovesherjob #makesomeonesday #essentialworkers

#protection

5) TurboTax: It went missing in action for a while today. We hunted and hunted, retraced our steps, and finally I pulled up my digital receipt to see what else I bought that day. I was hoping something would trigger it, and oh, yes, it was in the bag with the new hairdryer under the bathroom sink.

#electronicreceipts #thebomb

6) Funeral: Ellen was buried today. Her family grieved alone, during a beautiful but private Mass that was concelebrated by our three priests. It is heartbreaking to see my friend, her husband, and their children suffer this

tragic loss. Please embrace them and their family in your heart.

#tears #lonely #empty #somuchsadness

7) Wild turkey: A wild turkey strutted up my front yard, I guess seeking a shelter-in-place. At that moment, I was saying a small prayer for Ellen and her family. The sun was shining. The turkey came up, a light rain started, then stopped, and then the sun came back out.

#shivers #rainbow #protecther

8) Thanksgiving: The turkey reminded me that I still had some apple cranberry bars in the freezer. I have made these twice. Some recipes should just be left in the magazine.

#once #was enough #foolmetwice

9) Distracted: While we were having dinner, I looked up a recipe and sent a print request to the computer. After some point, I realized I was still hearing the printer. I now have 50 pages of reviews but not the recipe.

#sigh #carnitas

10) Sanitizing: While everyone is busy out there sanitizing their canned goods and other groceries, I'm here wondering how filthy my box of Saran wrap is that I have handled over the last 100 square feet of its life. Saved by the fact that it has been in my drawer well before the coronavirus reared its ugly head.

#washyourhands

Day 19

April 9, 2020

Gratitude:

1) My job. I can still get up and go to work every day.

2) Indoor geraniums.

3) Purple shoes. Red violet is the new purple.

4) Social distance yard art.

5) Cutco potato peeler.

6) Old school CD player with Johnny Cash playing.

7) A call from the church to see how we were doing during this Holy Week, if we needed anything, and if we had any prayer intentions.

8) Pajama pants at 3:18 pm followed with a Captain Morgan and Diet Coke.

9) Easter Egg surprises for the grocery store workers. They are my "first responders."

10) A phone call from my mom.

#lifeisbeautiful#doesnthavetobegrand

Day 20

Good Friday.

1) Good Friday is one of the holiest days in the Catholic religion, a day of fast and prayer. When we were kids, my siblings and I had a choice of either going to the Good Friday service in the afternoon or staying home to clean. I think I was 50/50 on the options. With the corona pandemic having shut every-thing down this year, there wasn't a decision to make.

   #clean #watchserviceontv

2) Church service: The Good Friday service was live streamed on YouTube. Watching in our living room and seeing an empty church feels so drastically strange for me. Yet, my son is "all in" during this shelter-in-place period. I guess observance/prayer does not necessarily have to happen inside a church.

   #myson #goodexample #uninhibited

3) Fast and abstinence: My husband and I have reached the age of exemption, but we still observe. It does not hurt us to hear a rumble

going on inside our stomach occasionally. The plus side of this being a day of fast and abstinence from meat, is that I pull out recipes I have been wanting to make, but never have gotten around to it. My mom had a system of saving notables on the inside of a cupboard door. I have apparently inherited that practice and took down the Seafood Lasagna recipe and asked my husband to go to the store to get the bay scallops. It took him two trips to the store, even though I mentioned "bay scallops" three times before he left the first time.

#cupboarddoors #betterthanarecipebox #notseascallops

4) Easter flowers: The fragrance in the air when passing the Easter lilies and hyacinths at the grocery store today was splendid! But do they last forever, like poinsettias? I am not taking that chance.

   #lilies #lasttoolong

5) Easter mail: We got an Easter card from my husband's aunt. We also got mail from Social Security.

   #buzzkill

6) Easter candy: I don't think it's possible, at least at our place, to have Easter without candy, but we are definitely skipping the baskets this year. The candy is holding steady at the store and I enjoy getting orders for requests with notes like "Peeps were my mom's favorites. I used to buy them on sale

after Easter and send several packages to her. It would drive my dad nuts!"

#nostalgia #joy #sendmejellybeans

7) Weather: It was a beautiful, sunny, fresh, and windy day. Not a day to worry about hairstyle!

#blowinginthewind

8) Shelter-in-place and Easter weekend: Sadly, it appears from the grocery store aisles that folks are prepping for Easter dinner . . . and company. We do not have shelter-in-place dispensation just because it is Easter weekend. There are still many people who are shopping single, but also many who are in pairs, or larger. We must observe the 6-foot-apart rule, even if we both need the Pillsbury biscuits at the same time!

#socialdistance

9) Radio: "Closing Time" is the final song on the morning show on Fridays. It always reminds me of the time my oldest son, Joe, and his friends wanted to do a parody of it at their senior Spring Pops Concert. It was going to be their take on closing out their high school career, but it got nixed. That would have been a fun song by his crazy friends.

#timetoclosethispost #endofgoodfriday

10) End: It just does not feel right to end a Top 10 list on an odd number or with less than a

complete list of ten. A list of 10 gives it balance, so now we have a #10.

#symmetry #closingtime

Day 21

April 11, 2020

Amusing myself on Day 21:

(Holy Saturday)

1) I am getting this post up before you are tucked in for the night or too sleepy to follow along!

    #stillawake

2) Good Friday and Holy Saturday used to mean some level of housekeeping when I was a kid. I am not sure why I always think cleaning the cupboard doors is a Holy Saturday job, but it is.

    #springcleaning

3) I became reacquainted with one of my best friends forever—the tub and tile cleaner! When that relationship didn't work out, I visited with the S.O.S. pad. That relationship had issues, too, but we made it work.

    #takesallkinds

4) I am still marveling that vacuum cleaner bags have been replaced by removable, plas-

tic canisters on newer models. All that dirt, though! Whew!

#goodsuction

5) It is great running into friends at the grocery store who remind me why I write these shelter-in-place updates. The friend I ran into today is yet another card-carrying member of the hypothetical "Don't Sweat the Small Stuff" club.

#shegetsittoo

6) I helped Matt get his audio and video on for the Zoom meeting with his Seabees leadership group. This is an amazing bunch of childhood cancer survivors who are now adults. There are some rough patches in their "neighborhood" right now. I am so grateful for the leader and her commitment to this kindred group.

#cancersucks

7) My husband found an old checkbook register from 1990 – 1991. Oh, how I miss the olden days and the local stores that are no longer open, like Magna, Union Hall, and Hilander.

#goodtimes

8) It is Saturday early evening, and I am waiting for 5:00 to roll around so the Lawrence Welk Easter special will come on. But then I

realized our cable company doesn't get that public broadcasting station anymore.

#hewasthebest #bigband #wunnerfulwunnerful

9) I ordered some flowers and had them delivered from a local flower shop. I am not sure how they are considered an essential business, but the flowers are beautiful.

#dingdongditch #doordrop

10) A friend thinks that the bishop is saying Mass via live stream tomorrow at 10:30 am. The bishop usually has Mass at the jail on holidays, so yeah, Mass could be interesting.

#hopeful #wontknowanyoneinjail

11) We ordered dinner from a local cantina and had beer from the pantry refrigerator that has clean crisper drawers that were washed the other day.

#orderout #easycleanup

12) Who's counting? Way over the 10-count limit!

#twoextratonight

Day 22

April 12,2020

Easter Sunday:

1) Happy Easter!

2) Shelter-in-place all day, save one order at the grocery store.

   #longstory #neededaluminumfoilanyway

3) I skipped the effort of digging out Easter baskets this year. Instead, I replaced that by using my Peter Rabbit Wedgewood china.

   #noonenoticed #ohbother

4) Our Easter dinner was at 1 p.m. Seven hours later and I am still full.

   #needagirdle #pjpantswork

5) I called my brother-in-law who lives in a group home in Chicago and they are totally shelter-in-place, too. He told me it was not the same without him with us. I will admit I laughed out loud when he said that. Of course, it's not the same without him. He totally rocks the 23rd chromosome.

   #downsyndrome

6) My brother-in-law also told me that the Superman socks I got him for Christmas have a hole in them.

#cueanewpair

7) The neighbors always put plastic eggs out in their yard. It is so pretty. I wonder how many kids out walking with their parents think it is an egg hunt.

#oops #empty

8) It might be time to wrap up these COVID-19 Top 10 lists. Who would have thought it would last so long?

#stayhome #washyourhands #killthisbeast

9) No number 9 tonight.

10) No number 10 tonight.

Day 23

April 13, 2020

Still here:

1) It is the twenty-third day since the governor ordered all nonessential businesses to close. The first thing I said to my husband this morning was, "I'd like the world to return to normal."

   #enoughsaid

2) The kids: Every single day I worry about the kids who are out of school. One of today's articles in the newspaper was spot on . . . how hard this is for parents, too. Now I can see my own bias and see hardships that many families experience daily, even when school is in session. The article was called "Can we have more empathy for low-income parents?" (estherjcepeda@washpost.com)

   #feedthem #housethem #lovethem #keepthemsafe

3) Grocery hustle: I didn't hit any garbage cans today, but I did notice a birthday message written on someone's car. It was written with a dry erase marker and wipes off with the rub of a finger. Who knew? Maybe I am "late to

the party" on this slick trick, but thought it was cool.

#windowstoo #cheapart

4) Masks: My cheeks are even chubbier when I wear my N95 mask. And earrings go AWOL quickly when taking it on and off so often.

#fakepearls #notlookingforit

5) McDonald's: The quip on my lid today was "Sip the Day." I first read it as "Skip the Day" and I thought what the heck?

#sneakyquip

6) Shelter-in-place project: We had some drawings done of our first home many years ago. Over time, the pictures slipped and needed to be re-matted. I needed some supplies to do that, including rubber cement. Oh, the amount of rubber cement I went through making teacher materials in college.

#bythequart #UNIdays #lovedaudiovisuallab

7) Easter candy: Chocolate can be irresistible, but do you really need to eat the whole bunny in one sitting? My husband suggested to Matt that he not eat all of it at once, so he didn't. He saved the tail for tomorrow.

#littlewillpower #wasntevenfanniemay
#norlindt #nordove

8) Dinner: I suck at making bacon. I do okay with fruit plates, but I do not need to make

Kodiak pancakes again. Whoever thought they were good for you?

#looklikeoatmealcookies #notoatmealcookies #notlikepancakeseither

9) Dinner themes: As I scrolled through my Facebook news feed, I saw that a friend's daughter is doing a different dinner theme each night this week. Tonight, it was chili and cornbread for cowboy night. They even dressed for dinner: boots, jeans, hats, belts, etc.

#lovethisidea #howfun #guesswhoscomingtodinner

10) Thanks for following along. I hope this wasn't "too long didn't read" (TLDR). I had to ask my daughter what TLDR meant.

#hangwithkids #learnstuff #TLDR

Day 24

April 14, 2020

Shelter-in-place continues:

1) Nothing life-changing occurred today until my McDonald's visit at mid-day. I thought a chocolate chip cookie would go great with my Diet Coke. "They aren't available during the pandemic." Well, shoot, then my family didn't get the other two sugar cookies, either.
   #caloriessaved #threeforadollar #suchadeal

2) Grocery hustle: The biggest news here is that Dawn dish soap and at least four brands of toilet paper were in stock today. That makes a shopper incredibly happy and as good as it gets today!
   #limittwo #cheapthrills

3) Daytime/nighttime TV: Even though I don't watch much TV . . . at all . . . I sat down for some of Kelly Clarkson and Ellen DeGeneres. I made it through the rest of Kelly's show, but fell asleep during Ellen's, even though she was as funny as always. Trying to get to a channel is the hardest part of watching

TV. I have not mastered working the remote control.

#standup #walktoTV #changechannel
#goodolddays

4) Coronavirus update/local "expert": The governor and then the county chairman do TV press conferences that cut into the Kelly Clarkson show. Matt faithfully watches the press conferences while waiting for the Kelly show. He is your guy if you want to know the current COVID situation.

#faithfulviewer #intheknow

5) Weather: Thankfully, there's flowers peeking through as the snow flurries flew.

#crazy #itisspringafterall

6) Dinner prep: My two favorite kitchen tools are the Dexas Grippmats and the Pampered Chef small tablespoon measuring cup.

#grippmats #blueischeese
#greenisvegetables #yellowispoultry
#redisbeef #whataboutpork

7) Hair: You would think women have it bad with outgrowth, bangs, etc., during the pandemic with all the salons being closed. But the men!

#mybrother #metamorphosis

8) Day 24 has been boring. You have probably taken a snooze after #2.

#sorry

9) Social distancing: It matters.
#keepitup

10) Masks: All sorts and kinds. It matters.
#wearone

Day 25

April 15, 2020

Happy Birthday to my daughter and my mother-in-law!

1) Birthdays: We brought my daughter into this world on my mother-in-law's birthday. Carrie is 24 and my dear mother-in-law is 93. My daughter was born at the height of our most challenging time and was embraced with so much love and support. Grandmas, aunts, uncles, friends, and neighbors all took turns helping with her and Joe, who was then four years old, while my husband and I were totally overwhelmed with our two-year-old's cancerous brain tumor. Matt's treatment and care seemed all-consuming, but we were surrounded with angels. One of Matt's overnight home health nurses made Carrie's first birthday cake. Today Carrie made her own! One of Carrie's first words was "boon" (balloon) and once she started crawling, her favorite toys were the heparin flush bottles for Matt's central venous line that were stored under the buffet.

#love #triumph

2) Masks: I am not sure why I bother to use the curling iron on my hair in the morning since the on/off with a mask wreck it anyway. I further question myself when I start to use the curling iron and I realize I had forgotten to turn it on.

#tellingmesomething

3) Grocery hustle: It is interesting to notice which businesses are open as I drive down some of the main streets in town. Menard's? It is packed today! What the heck? Were they running a 5/$10.00 sale on Jack's frozen pizzas again?

#lasttimeiwasthere #pizzasfromthehardwarestore #nowthatisweird

4) Radio: I really like Riley Green's song "I Wish Grandpas Never Died" but today when it came on, I automatically said to myself, "I wish kids never died." One of my daughter's high school classmates died in a car accident last night. She was a buddy in our Buddy Baseball program besides so many other beautiful things. May her light shine.

#Eliana

5) McDonald's: I secretly smile when I pick the drive through-lane that gets served before the other one.

#imnotcompetitive

6) Daytime TV: I usually get home from my grocery shopping gig about 3 or 3:30 p.m.

I still think Phil Donahue or Oprah Winfrey should come on at 4:00.

#thatwasawhileago

7) Conversation at the dinner table: We asked one another what we would take if we (god-forbid) had a house fire. My daughter said she would take her Kitchen Aid mixer. I said I would take my son.

#withoutadoubt

8) E-learning: We are still struggling. We were so frustrated and stuck that I asked on Facebook for some help. A former classmate of Matt's and an old colleague came to the rescue. We are still not up and running, but not giving up.

#labclass #athome #ishard #dontknowthesoftware

9) Stimulus checks: My kids have received theirs. They are truly adulting now!

#blinkblink

10) Themed Dinners: I am waiting for my friend to post her family's dinner picture for tonight. I am guessing it is a Fiesta theme.

#hurryupsara #funstuff #covid19creativity

Day 26

April 16, 2020

Top 10 accomplishments today:

1) I perked up a droopy tulip within 30 minutes by dropping a penny in the water. Really, that does work!

   #imnotkidding

2) I served as an accomplice to successfully getting Matt's video/Vimeo submitted to his professor for his class.

   #relieved #highfive

3) I sewed the string back on a disposable mask so I can wear it again tomorrow while I wait for my order to come in.

   #desperate

4) I breathed a sigh of relief and rested easy when the car behind me was only a hospital courtesy car and not the police, so I went ahead and finished the business on my phone at the stoplight.

   #spared #stayoffyourphone

5) I relived some delicious memories of hearing my high school friends call me "Sheri O." A customer drew a smile face next to my name on the thank you note she left for me and it looked like Sheri O.

#maidenname #startedwitho

6) With great willpower, I resisted eating my sack lunch in the car at 10:00. Instead, I ate the apple and only two Doritos Cool Ranch chips.

#mindovermatter

7) The monthly meeting of the Patient Family Advisory Council for Swedish American Hospital was held through Webex for the first time instead of in-person. This was new for all of us and it worked well. We heard how the hospital is responding to COVID-19 cases, triaging, managing supplies, etc. It was interesting, fascinating, and reassuring. The "incident command central" at the hospital is a buzz of activity and it's encouraging to hear how our three local hospitals are collaborative partners in this pandemic.

#togetherisstronger #allforone #teamwork

8) I exercised today! I dropped off a thermometer for a friend and climbed his two flights of stairs twice to ensure he was ok.

#bigworkout #justkidding

9) We had Easter leftovers for dinner and the mashed potatoes are finally gone. But that ham, will it ever end?

   #oinkoink

10) I explained the "birds and the bees" in very concrete terms today to my son. I thought he knew all this stuff; it was clear he did not.

   #explain #discuss #repeat

Day 27

April 17, 2020

Prepping for the weekend:

1) It is Friday but still SSDD: same stuff, different day. We are still asked to shelter-in-place, and apparently will be for much longer. One big difference about today from the past 26 days though, is that the blooming daffodils were in a bed of snow this morning and they were not in March.

   #seasonsareconfused

2) A friend who is a retired preschool teacher and now a happy grandma did not miss a beat and filled up a bucket of snow for some inside fun with her grandson.

   #frosty #isinthehouse

3) Masks: It does not matter if there's parsley or broccoli in your teeth from your lunch. No one will notice.

   #masked

4) Impromptu happy hours are the best and since there isn't any place to go anyway, why not have one at home? My husband said

"Get a nice bottle of Merlot," and we invited a friend up.

#notafanofmerlot #neverknowwhattoget
#pourmeabeerinstead

5) Liquor departments in grocery stores are often much nicer than many liquor stores. Some older liquor stores give me the creeps and smell funny.

#needupgrades #lesspinesol

6) I thought my favorite kitchen tools were the Grippmats and the tiny measuring cup until I needed the reaching claw (grabber) tonight. Happy Hour requires baskets to put snacks in and they were too far out of reach in the cupboards. I love that grabber thing!

#souvenir #disneyworld #alongtimeago

7) Happy Hour also requires alcohol. Oh, Lordy, I need a liquor cabinet or someone to weed out the nonessentials on these pantry shelves, so it becomes a masterpiece of organization.

#multipurposeroom #firstaidsupplies
#randomstuff #liquorbottles #itsamess

8) Our dinner menu tonight was take-out. This is a great break from the time spent fixing a meal to the time spent consuming it.

#disproportionate #lentisover
#orderfromsmokeybones #bbq

9) I thought shelter-in-place would be short and we would do something together each night That lasted four nights.

#Mayberryopoly #5Secondrule
#Yahtzee #KingsCorner

10) It is going to be the weekend all weekend long. Follow the rules, there isn't any place to go anyway. Do something different like vacuum behind your bed, order pictures from your camera roll, delete old word documents, sort your personal library and set books aside for trading or donating, open a cookbook to a random page and make something from it, sort your sock drawer, use your Voice Memo app to record someone's voice you love, throw out old pens that don't work and pencils that have crappy erasers. Need more ideas? Let me know.

#stayhome #thistooshallpass

Day 28

April 18, 2020

Today's crazies:

1) Artwork: I wrote my name in the dust on the piano.

   #artwork #nowthenewdusting

2) Radio: I heard the "Stay Home" song by Big and Rich.

   #prettyfunny #shelterinplace

3) Masks: I'm wondering if I have been wearing my disposable masks inside out. In fact, I have been obsessing over it since some friends and I were talking about it the other day. Is the blue side the inside or the outside?

   #doesitreallymatter #covid19query

4) Lunch: Eating leftovers was the plan but instead we ordered Chinese and had to call two restaurants to place an order. The first one had a recording that said, "We are temporarily closed due to lack of supplies." I guess they shop at Meijer just like the rest of us and have stock problems.

   #butitisgettingbetter

5) I accomplished a real shelter-in-place project today. The pantry has been overhauled and all the liquor bottles are on the same shelf.

   #beatthat

6) My guys like coffee and use a Keurig machine. However, the K-cup boxes don't collapse well for recycling and this really bugs me!

   #pantrywork #firstworldproblems

7) It is amazing what a glass bowl will do to dress up Christmas and Valentine candy in April. It looks so much prettier in a glass bowl than in random Ziploc bags that are stuffed here and there on a pantry shelf.

   #garbageonmonday #throwcandyout #oreatit

8) During dinner preparation I discovered a new way to drain pineapple rings. Hang the pineapple on a handle of a fork or wooden spoon while it drips into a bowl and ta-da, you don't need a strainer.

   #savethestrainer #kitchenhack

9) In McDonald's Diet Coke news today, my lid said "Aaahh Tasty" on it. On occasion, orders get messed up and they hand me a regular Coke or a tea. I was reminded of all the times we got wrong orders at the drive-through in my small Iowa hometown. Things weren't always so "aaahh tasty" when you took a drink of something and it's not what you thought it was going to be.

   #notfunnythen #funnynow #dietcokeplease

10) I asked my guys to arbitrarily pull a cookbook off the top shelf, open it to any page and pick a recipe. Tomorrow's menu includes tortellini with creamy parmesan dipping sauce and blueberry refrigerator pie. Good thing they sort of complement each other.

#churchcookbooks #kidsschoolcookbook

Day 29

Randomness:

1)   I just wanted to sit in my pantry all day on one of the little step stools stored there and admire the fabulous make-over from yesterday. I could have used the claw tool to reach the basket and eat snacks while I marveled at my work.

#whileawaythehours #impressedmyself

2)   Chips-Ahoy cookies are a mediocre substitute for a homemade chocolate chip cookie.

#onlyinapinch

3)   I always thought "Shelter in Place" looked funny when I typed it, and thanks to a friend's post tonight, I see that it needs hyphens, and it looks much better! This friend is used to hyphens. She has one in her name. My maiden name with 14 letters would be much too long to hyphenate.

#hyphens #makewordslookgood

#sherioberbroecklingwhite #shelter-in-place

4) Having church on TV in the living room is hard. I think I could attend better in the car as a podcast. After our local 10:00 Mass, we switched over to the Basilica of the National Shrine of the Immaculate Conception in Washington, DC for a few minutes. We loved that church when we visited several years ago so it was good to see it again. It was interesting to note their choir of six people was standing 6 feet apart.

#socialdistancing #evenatchurch

5) My son routinizes well. Matt has continued his walks on an almost daily basis even though the YMCA closed because of the pandemic. He walks for 60 minutes. Sometimes 65. If it is beyond that, my worry radar goes off. Matt knows several of the neighbors so I can always check in with them to see if they have seen him. When he gets back, he mentions who he saw and who said to say hello to me.

#iphonefunction #findmyphone #activateit

6) The marketing department must have thought they were funny (or mean) when they placed Clorox products on the first page of the Sunday newspaper coupons. You couldn't buy them if you wanted to.

#stillsoldout

7) My day was sweetened when I found a cute pansy on my kitchen counter when I got

back from work. My friend Karen was out sending smiles today.

#spreadjoy #surprisesomeone

8) I screwed up the one grocery order I did today. There was a quart Ball canning jar on the list. I checked it out with the order but knew when I delivered, I did not have the jar. I made another 15-mile round trip to get the jar and drop it off. It was a nice day for a drive, I guess.

#theysellsinglejars #sundaydrive
#oldpeopledothat #gasischeap

9) To be honest, the Michael Jordan special that started tonight appeals to me . . . a little. Just enough to know what people are talking about. Five Sunday nights x 2 hours each night equals a lot of TV watching to which I am not accustomed.

#iwilltry #itmightbegood

10) This list doesn't have a #10 tonight. When your younger sister says it's ok if you don't have ten every night, you believe her. Who is counting, anyway?

#lowexpectations #verylazytoday

Day 30

April 20, 2020

6:00 a.m. start:

1) My phone starts chiming at 6:00 each morning, sending offers through the app for grocery orders for the day. The demand has been staggering and the phone chimes continually for a few seconds. Unknowingly, I snapped a picture of my old-school clock radio right at 6:00 on the button as I reached for my phone. I didn't even know I did it until I checked my camera roll tonight.

   #getup #gotowork #iamlucky

2) I am out of facial moisturizer. That sucks. I had to start the day with my night cream. Looks like tomorrow morning will be a repeat.

   #callthemarykaylady

3) People are still throwing their disposable gloves on the ground at the grocery store. This is so disgusting and maddening. Conventional wisdom seems to be leaning towards not wearing gloves, anyway.

   #noteffective #spreadsgerms

#washyourhands #usesanitizer

4)   It is garbage day in the northeast part of my city. I only had one obstacle course today in a driveway and there was just the right amount of width to exit the driveway without clobbering the cans.

#feelingaccomplished

5)   My husband's "work at home" arrangement has been a benefit to me in several ways.

*#luncheswithourson #loadsdishwasher
#doeslaundry #stilldoesntdowindows*

6)   Meal prep is going well this week. Ha! I had two nights planned and still needed my husband to run to the store for mustard seed and a few other things. The jar of roasted peanut simmer sauce is not great!

#tooplain #mustardseedforsomethingelse

7)   All day I made a mental note to be sure I did not mention food once in this post tonight.

#itsnotpossible

8)   To-do lists are one of my favorite things each day. You would think my success rate would be better since all I do is go to work and stay home. A sympathy card is almost ready for the mail. My contacts are ordered. My drive-through appointment at the bank is scheduled. Getting new facial moisturizer is still on the list.

#tomorrow #anotherday

9) I checked in on my mom yesterday. She loves her apartment in the senior living community and the corner unit with a balcony. Yay for sunshine! Yay for fresh air! Yay for the maintenance man taking a break from time to time and chatting with her.

   #seniorliving #shelovesit

10) Now that the pantry is overhauled, it's time to use up some of those half-empty bottles and mix up some sangria.

   #brandy #vodka #grenadine #cheers

Stay safe. We are still under pressure. We will get there.

Day 31

Carry on: shelter-in-place:

1) Sydney, Australia seems to have figured out how to deal with bars shutting down. They can now deliver cocktails.

   #itmustbetrue #thepapersaidso #immovingtoaustralia

2) It's also true that a friend of mine is right. "Some of our houses will still be a complete mess when the stay-at-home ban is lifted. And I don't even care if you judge me."

   #truth #mykindofphilosophy

3) My lipstick usage is way down. I hope when this is all over and we're not wearing masks anymore I will find the tube that is missing in action in my car.

   #eventuallyturnsup #pursespills

4) I have a hole in each ear. They are usually covered with earrings. I have given up wearing them while wearing a mask.

   #cryuncle

5) I felt rich today. I filled my tank with the middle grade gasoline for $1.75/gallon.

#twentytwodollars #fulltank

6) "We" made summer sausage today. I prepared it and my husband took it out of the oven.

#mentioningfoodagain #highschoolbandcookbook

7) In some ways I think we have taken this social distancing thing too far. Cars are sometimes 6 feet apart . . . in the drive-through lines and at stoplights. My oldest son told me that is how he learned it in driver's ed.

#movealong

8) My husband is a TV watcher, but I am not. Yet, I find myself being drawn into the commercials by corporate America on staying home.

#allthefeels #differentthansuperbowl #verygood

9) I think some of the parents are implementing art class by having kids draw appreciation pictures for their grocery shopper. I got two today.

#milkandcookies #inthepicture #amiSanta

10) Last truth of the day: I am out of wildly exciting experiences to share.

#cuetaps #dayisdone

Carry on, friends, we have a lot of week left to shelter-in-place.

Day 32

April 22, 2020

Signs of the coronavirus:

1) My workday is spent primarily at the Meijer grocery super store, a chain store throughout the Midwest. The company has evaluated and worked to clean/sanitize/remove/replace all things that have high-level touch points in the building. One of the produce workers was carrying a metal Stanley coffee thermos, the kind my dad used to carry in his lunch box. I thought she was much too young to carry a Stanley, so I asked her about it.

    #removedthecoffeepots #employeebreakroom
    #coffeepothandles #touchpoints
    #shebringsherowncoffeenow

2) There was a senior woman standing by the case of fresh chicken today and I couldn't help but notice the two gallons of wine in her cart. If you are inviting her to your Bring Your Own Booze party when the shelter-in-place is lifted, I think she will be staying awhile.

    #meatballsincart #appetizer #inviteher

3) Occasionally I must buy groceries for ourselves, like everyone else. You know, the kind where the cart gets full and you add things with reckless abandon. Aisle 12 where I shop is the Sinner's Aisle. Cookies, cookies, and more cookies. I believed the label on a package of cookies that read: If you're going to have a cookie, have a COOKIE.

#pepperidgefarm #tahoe #cookiesduringcoronoa

4) This has nothing to do with signs of the coronavirus, but it is something I want to share with you. "Tookie" was one of the last words my two-year old son said the night before his brain tumor surgery. He was prepped for surgery so he couldn't eat that night. It was hard to distract him. It was a year later when Matt had his next "tookie." We love our "tookies."

#Oreoswithgrandpa #survivor

5) Things don't necessarily move at lightning speed here at our place just because we're home. The sympathy card I started yesterday will go out in the mail tomorrow. Whitepages. com isn't as user-friendly as it used to be, but a friend saved the day by finding the address I needed.

#herchurchdirectory

6) We really do need to keep our wits and sense of humor about us during these trying and "unprecedented" times. I got my giggles today from a meme on Facebook: Is COVID-19 REALLY that serious? Listen y'all, the

casinos and churches are closed. When heaven and hell AGREE on the same thing, it is probably pretty serious.

#saferathome #laugherisgoodforthesoul

7) Trivia is a thing. A thing I am not particularly good at. The local Better Business Bureau set up an "815 Takeout and Dine-In" event tonight—order take out from a local business and play trivia with others on Facebook Live or Zoom, while tucked safely at home. We scored 16/30. I knew two answers.

#crazyquestions #notmything #ilikeyahtzee

8) Everyone is Zooming. One of my brothers set us up tonight and at one point I had three devices going to make sure I'd get it right: the desktop computer, my son's iPad, and my phone. Scratch the desktop, it doesn't have a camera or microphone.

#obsoletetechnology #noaccessories

9) Copy and paste should still be my Best Friend Forever.

#learnthehardway

10) It is 11:29 pm. Why am I not in bed? Because I didn't copy and paste this list when I was on #6 and I "left this page" on Facebook to do something else and lost all of it.

#retyped #ohmygoodness #toolatetoproof

I'm not sure if this is "good night" or "good morning" but thanks for reading.

Day 33

April 23, 2020

On the home front:

1) Press Conference: The governor announced today that we will stay put until May 3, 2020. My husband muttered something under his breath that should not be repeated here. His work is approximately 60% field-based so sitting at home in a make-shift office is tough for him.

#saferathome #noteasythough #wecandoit

2) My son has been off work for about a month although he seems to fill his time well enough. When I asked Matt if he missed work, he said it was "different." Different because he could watch TV all afternoon now. (shaking my head) My husband thinks he misses his life.

#weallmissourlives

3) Wii Golf: My guys were Wii golfing when I got home late this afternoon. Happy hour had already started so I just could not help myself and had to admire my reorganized pantry and pour myself a little something

from one of the bottles in the dedicated corner with the alcohol.

#prohibitionislongover

4) Amazon: Matt is probably the best online shopper at our place. My husband was helping him check out an order today and was shocked to see he was spending a tidy sum on a CD. He looked to see if it was coming from an international seller. Nope, just southern California. From my eavesdropping chair in the other room, I casually mentioned that Matt hasn't been spending any money lately: no Subway, Papa John's, or Meg's coffee shop while at Rock Valley College, no Para Transit bus tickets, no Uber rides, and no theater tickets. So, they clicked on "place order" and you can bet Matt will be first to grab the mail the day the CD is due to arrive.

#discretionaryfunds #livealittle #mailisfun #iamhisreppayee #shesaidok

5) Mail: Some is welcomed, some is not. We have been inundated with return address labels and note pads from agencies as a "Thank you for your donation." Like, who sends out mail anymore, at least not dozens and dozens of stuff every few days? There's no way we could ever use up all of these mail labels.

#chairitablecauses #memorialgifts #mailinglists

6) More mail: It was a big mail day today! Besides more mail labels, the masks I ordered arrived. Oh, Lordy! Looks like a mask, cov-

ers like a mask, but I do not think it's effective as a mask.

#theywerecheap #seenumber7

7) Masks: I can't even on some of them! I heard that someone was wearing a turtleneck and pulled it up over their nose and mouth. But the best one I heard about was someone wearing a sleep shade as a mask. I laughed so hard I had to stop and catch my breath!

#asleepshade #overyourmouthandnose #nowthatsfunny

8) Phone: It is odd when the phone rings anymore AND it is actually a real person and someone you haven't talked to in a long time!! It was so great to hear from a former colleague and a good friend.

#surprisesurprisesurprise

9) Relationships are always a work in progress and now we have lots of time to work on those. But none are any better than the romance between two elderly people in Germany and Denmark. My friend sent a great story on "border" love. They hold hands by sitting on either side of the border line.

#lovebirds #socialdistancing

10) Feet: It's time to wrap this post up because my feet are cold and it's #10 anyway!

#saygoodnight #saygoodnightjohnboy #thewaltons #neverwatchedit

It has been really hard to keep the days straight this week. Things are getting muddled. I'll have to pin a note to the inside of my sleeve to remind me. Hang in there, we are on an upward climb.

Day 34

Essentials for shelter-in-place:

1) Memory: Remembering that you've got fresh produce to use before it gets brown.

   #packalunch #cauliflower #eatincar #emptyparkinglots

2) Recipes: I like trying out different things to add some flair to the day. Even though I have been invited to join a quarantine recipe exchange, I don't have the motivation. My chain letter days ended around 1968 after writing one letter to the name on top of the list, adding five new people and expecting to get 36 letters in return. Ha! That was a bust.

   #fishtacos #tonight #seasoningpacket #simple

3) Dishwasher soap/pods: I can't believe how often we're running the dishwasher compared to when we weren't under the shelter-in-place order. We are not used to having breakfast, lunch and dinner dishes every day.

   #paperplates #rareforus

4) Vacuum cleaner: There's so much more foot traffic through the family room with everyone home. I am vacuuming so much more often than usual.

#retractablecord #nextvacuum #nonnegotiable

5) Laundry baskets: These are multi-use containers. Besides the obvious, they serve as a deposit box for delivering groceries at the doorstep to maintain "no contact" practices, and turned upside down transform into a mobile desk while a phone is charging in my family room, and triples as a footrest while scrolling through Facebook after the phone has charged.

#souseful #rubbermaid #arethebest

6) Fresh bread: I applaud all of you successful bakers out there who have been baking bread. As for me, I inhaled the amazing smell at Great Harvest today and called it good.

#iamyeast #flunky

7) Plumber: A vehicle with the license plate "Plunger" was in front of me today. We didn't need him, but I bet the person who did was grateful that this is an essential service.

#HalsPlumbing #thebestfolks

8) Envy: Realizing some of your peeps are getting a whole lot more done during shelter-in-place than you'd even think about doing. Where is that to-do list I mentioned a few

days ago? I took off the Easter mailbox cover yesterday. That should count for something.

#getbusy #overwhelmed #makeaplan

9) Celebrations: A little fun fact about the work I do; I shopped my 3500th order today! So, I said, "yay me" and had a "Peach on the Beach" frozen drink and pretended I was on the beach in Mexico with my sisters again.

#thatwasfun #thelittlethings

10) Compassion: While we may be feeling detached, lonely, isolated, missing out, sad, etc., don't forget there's others who are dealing with the effects of the coronavirus or grieving someone very close to them. Send the card, write the note, text a message, drop something off, say a prayer, Facetime or Zoom with them.

#dosomething

Here we go, the weekend starts! I think I'll get out the scissors and shelf liner and see if anything happens with it.

Day 35

April 25, 2020

Stayed home (mostly):

Like most people, I was home most of today since I only worked for a few hours. But it started out in the garage . . .

1) 7:00 am: You know how it is when you can't find something, and your mind doesn't settle until it's found? I knew it had to be somewhere and the last place it could be was in my husband's car from the summer. Yep, there it was. And it has been so long that I've been in his car since shelter-in-place that I thought it still had that new car smell.

    #2018Rav4 #didntevenneed #whatifound #goodgrief #peacefulmind

2) 7:45 am: I told a friend where her husband could find the frozen drink beverages at Meijer that I posted yesterday. Without giving her exact latitude and longitudinal degrees, I gave her living color pictures so he could locate them easily and find the right thing. Because, you know, guys do not like to ask for help.

    #margaritahunt #zoomcocktailparty

3) 12:30 pm: By this time, I was well overdue for a Diet Coke . . . and the line was long. I quickly opened the straw at the drive-through window to taste my drink, because sometimes they get it wrong when they are busy. Yes, it was wrong, again. The drive-through gal then gave me my correct order of a Diet Coke, but I had to keep the regular Coke, too. My husband had some of it with his Jack's pizza lunch.

#jumpforjoy #niceonice

4) 1:30 pm: I gave myself a mani-pedi. Los Cabos Coral was the color on the top (fingernails) and Nomad's Dream was the color on the bottom (toenails). That little toe though . . . the tip of the toe gets as much polish on it as the toenail. We need to get those stylists, barbers, manicurists, etc., back to work!

#weneedyou #essentialworkerstoo #pros

5) 2:30 pm: I checked Facebook and was thrilled to see a friend and his wife had their baby yesterday.

#babiesaremiracles #birthingismiraculous

6) 3:00 pm: Old people might call bank statement reconciliation bookkeeping. I call it crazy. But there I am, three or four times a year, poring over paper statements and checking off transactions in my checkbook. I don't have OCD, but that is one compulsion

I can't break. I don't bother reconciling it, I just check off the debits and credits.

#neverreconciles #doitanyway
#needthatclosure #nuts

7) 4:45 pm: I needed to go to CVS for some things before my coupons expired. I tried hard not to listen to a customer rip the clerk/manager about masks or something. Honestly, I didn't hear all of it, but it was uncalled for, whatever it was.

#rude #covid19 #bekind

8) 5:45 pm: Multi-tasking is something I am pretty good at, especially while making dinner: prepare chicken and dumplings, line a few shelves with new shelf-liner, mix up some sangria, load the dishwasher, and check the internet to learn more about dumplings. I don't think Jiffy pancake mix is the same as Bisquick.

#oops #workedfine #alittlesweeter
#tasteslikechicken

9) 6:15 pm: That darn nail polish started chipping off already. I have not learned how to work in the kitchen and have painted nails.

#notopcoat #stubbynails #anyway

10) 7:45 pm: It is Saturday night, so we lived it up by playing a card game called Garbage. For real, that is what it is called. My son smoked us.

#fun #easy #fast #googleit.

How many more weekends to go? Too many!

Day 36

April 26, 2020

Sunday:

1) Oh yes, we are still wearing masks. I stepped out of the car this morning and saw someone wearing a mask. For a nanosecond, I forgot we were still doing that. I went back to the car to put that itchy thing on.

   #killjoy #niceday

2) Masks have become a fashion show. The prints apparently speak the person's passions.

   #awkward #staringatstrangers

3) Shopping is meant to be a solo enterprise during shelter-in-place. Please remind your friends and neighbors. Honor the store's procedures.

   #shopalone #onepershoppingcart

4) Mother Nature does not discriminate. The season is changing despite shelter-in-place.

   #washthewintercoats #airtheblankets

5) It has been another Sunday to take advantage of going to church "somewhere" else. I chose

Franciscan University for today's Mass.

#steubenvilleohio #sonsalmamater
#livingroom #notthesame

6) You know I love a good cookie and have complete admiration for those who can decorate cut-outs. Today I saw some that were amazing and fun—toilet paper rolls, martini glasses, and virus spikey balls.

#coronavirus #cutoutcookies #creative

7) "Jose Cuervo" (Shelly West, 1983) was my favorite song on the radio today. The oldies take me back to a time when our lives were a bit more carefree.

#ohthememories #covid19willhavememoriestoo

8) My husband fired up the Weber for our first burgers on the grill this season. I pulled out a cookbook and used up the cottage cheese and blackberry jello and made a recipe out of the first St. Bridget School cookbook. The recipe is called "cottage cheese jello stuff." It is an appropriate title because that's exactly what it is.

#goodforpotlucks #funeraldinnersalad

9) Tomorrow's shelter-in-place goal: Write it without hashtags.

#hashtags #summarize #succinctly

10) No #10.

#bored

Day 37

April 27, 2020

Monday to do list:

1) Retrieve letter stencils from the basement to make a poster for a four-year-old's birthday parade.

Done.

#teachermaterials #neverdie #theyjustgotoclosettorest

2) Set up and explain the stencil tracing and cutting project to my son.

Done.

#teacheraide #greathelp #birthdayposter

3) Collect all the glue sticks from the top drawer and pitch the dry ones.

Done.

#fiveweregood #twotothetrash

4) Plan a road trip to the Village Bakery in Oregon, IL for tomorrow.

Done.

#supportlocalbusiness #placeorder

#drivethrough #employpeoplewithdisabiities
#cookiesandbread #carepackages

5) Arrange to drop off an item for my sister-in-law in Oregon tomorrow.

Done.

#viewBlackHawkstatue #fromheryard

6) Make a note to get a home-town paper in Byron, IL or Oregon, IL tomorrow.

Done.

#toomanycovidarticles #ourlocalpaper
#Chicagopaper #smalltownstories
#weddinganniversaries #goodneighborstories
#seewhosecowsorgoatsgotout
#tractorparades #ilovesmalltownpapers

7) Notice that some people's masks could be intimidating or even scary under "normal" conditions.

Done.

#clowningaround #masksruntherange

8) Read an article in the Chicago Tribune.

Done.

#DIYmasks #cottonisbest #duh #stillinteresting

9) Remove nail polish that was applied 2 days ago. Not done. Reschedule for tomorrow.

#applycolorstreetadhesivenails #dontgiveup

10) Call Mom. Not done. Reschedule for Tues. or Wed.

#brothercallsher #mondaynights

11) Mail nagging paperwork. Not done. Reschedule for Tues.

#inenvelope #stamped #mailboxinthemorning

12) Don't use hashtags. Not done. Reschedule for tomorrow.

#hashtags #soeasy #makesyouthink #decode

Day 38

The Village Bakery, Oregon IL:

1) So many things to love about The Village Bakery and Oregon, IL!

   a) They took my $75.00 order over the phone and didn't require prepayment. Your word is good at the Village Bakery.

   b) They have a timely and interactive Facebook page.

   c) The order was completely ready at the designated time and they also added extra twist ties to portion out the goodies.

   d) The packaging for transporting was superb.

   e) They are an extension of the sheltered workshop and employ people with disabilities.

   f) It has high visibility in downtown Oregon.

   g) It is apparent the community supports it well.

h) The drive down Route 2 on a sunny day with my son was glorious.

i) The town has so many beautiful homes.

j) It makes me feel like I am at home in Dyersville, IA.

2) In other news, I asked Matt during dinner what his top three things were about today. Surely, I thought the trip to Oregon would be #1. Ha! The Kelly Clarkson and Ellen DeGeneres shows were on his list. The car ride or the bakery did not make his list at all. To his credit, he did mention the walk we took around the village square in Oregon.

3) I had really wanted to go to this bakery but sort of planned it for a day out for Matt. I even changed the country radio station in the car to the pop music station. He turned down the radio to have a video chat with his (girl) friend and then opened his blue-ray player.

4) We have had a long-time practice of packing the portable DVD/blue-ray player when we'd have trips to Madison, WI for Matt's doctor appointments. Even though we don't have those appointments anymore, he still packs the equipment for "long" car rides. Before we left for our 50-minute trip, I asked him if he had everything he needed for it, including the car charger. He said yes. I ask him every single time before we go. Every single time he does not have everything he needs. It makes me so crazy! I pulled off the winding road along the river to check the bag and nope,

not there. I try the power switch, the play button, and the mode button. I cannot get it to work. I calmly tell him I can't get it. I want to tell him, "Suck it up, buddy, enjoy the ride and the beautiful scenery."

5) I stopped at the Mobil gas station in Byron for a local paper. There were two headlines. The lesser one was about the United Way and fund allocation for COVID-19 emerging needs. The major headline in bold type was "Pig Tales: Students Learn about Swine with Ag in the Classroom" with a full color picture of a little girl smiling from ear to ear. There ya have it, folks: good, local news. Living everyday life!

6) I fixed up some care packages with the treats from the bakery for my neighbors and made a shelter-in-place welfare check. I spotted them on their front porch a short while later having a cup of coffee with the cookies I brought and enjoying the downpour. Too sweet!

7) This list got long. I have had two tall glasses of homemade sangria tonight. I guess I got a little chatty.

8) There are no hashtags tonight and I survived.

9) We don't need a #9 and #10. There is a bonus with #1.

Day 39

April 29, 2020

Things to know today that (won't) change your world:

1) My favorite lounging clothes are a pair of Joe Boxer fleece pants from the now closed Kmart store and my blue Buddy Baseball sweatshirt from my brother's program in Florida. The colors match. I am a fashion statement. Even at 4:00 in the afternoon.

2) When you don't call your mom, she eventually calls you after her standing 2:00 Wednesday afternoon on-line euchre game with her hometown friends.

3) Some of the guys on the TV programs that my husband watches have the weirdest mustaches, goatees, beards, and sideburns. He even agrees with me, which is a little unusual.

4) A friend of mine is making dinner for her daughter's family once a week during the month of May as a Mother's Day gift. I love this idea! I wish my kids lived closer!

5) There was still a bag of jellybeans in the bottom drawer. I don't know if they were the

99-cent bag after Easter sale or the 2/$4.00 ones before Easter. I save the black ones for my husband.

6) We ordered dinner tonight from Anna's Pizza, a local restaurant. This is the kind of place you have driven by so many times but never noticed. My son notices these places but, in this case, it is across from where he works so he's seen it often.

#supportlocalbusiness #eatpizza

7) No matter how long you work on some things, they just don't work out. No need to read into this. It is nothing serious. It's like dusting . . . it just has to be done again and again. In fact, I think I would pay someone to dust for me.

8) Things are looking good at the grocery store. People are generally shopping alone and wearing masks. The blue tape on the floor to mark aisle traffic direction wasn't all that effective, but it could be totally cool on the weekend if the crowds follow it!

9) I'm just about over this rain.

10) You can tell I am stretching to fill this list. No expectations, I know, but I can't leave my list hanging without having a complete set of 10. It just does not work.

#imalittlecrazy #notmanyhashtags #didyounotice

Day 40

April 30, 2020

It's been 40 days! We're still here.

1) Domestic conundrums: I have wondered more than once if it matters which side is up when you place the pod in the dishwasher. Does the plain side or the shiny side with Dawn in it go face up? I go with the shiny side because that seems to be the "top." Also, I roll my eyes when the hairspray doesn't come close to reaching your hair because the nozzle has been pasted over with gunk.

   #usebobbypins #cleaningoutgunk #firstworldproblems

2) Radio: My favorite song on the radio today was "Downtown" (Petula Clark, 1964). It reminded me of how envious I was of Patty's white go-go boots in second grade. Oh, how I loved those boots. It also made me think of how great it will be when the shelter-in-place is lifted, and we can all go downtown and enjoy life again.

   #notholdingmybreath #anytimesoon #thosebootsthough

3) McDonald's: Relatively speaking, the lines have been short in the drive-through during the last several weeks. But now they are picking up it seems. I made a sandwich for lunch today and it was almost gone before it was my turn to order. Then I had to pretty much guzzle my pop because it was almost time to go back to work and put my mask back on.

#swishandswallow #dentalhygiene
#backingradeschool #siptheday
#theyneednewinspirations #lids

4) Career change: I made a major career change after only five years of teaching in the classroom. I went to a large residential agency and ran their developmental day training program. I met and worked with a lot of people during that time. It was the highlight of my day today when a shopper/former colleague of mine told me I was the nicest boss when we worked together. Now how sweet was that? That was so many years ago!!

#allthefeels #makesomeonesday

5) More on that time period: As she and I chatted, I told her about some of the times I had to fire people. One person told me I was "cold" when I terminated her. (Honey, this was not warm and fuzzy for either of us!) Another time, well past when I had left that job, a guy called me out at a grade school registration and said "Hey, Sheri . . . do you remember when you fired me?" (and all the people milling about could hear). I said, "Oh, my gosh, really?" He said, "Yes, and it

was the best thing you could've done because I really needed my a** kicked then!" And there he stood, proudly introducing me to his wife and family.

#makesomeonesday #iguess

6) Masks: A friend kidded on Facebook that fuzzy dice hanging from the car mirror are "so last year" and now the trendiest rear-view mirror accessories are face masks. Mine doesn't look like hers.

#hersareclean #lorealallovermine

7) Worker bees: Two of my favorite helpers when I deliver their groceries have cute face masks that their mom made them. The last time I saw them they had winter scarves wrapped around their nose and mouth. Not today. Today they had their favorite sports team on their masks.

#tshirtmasks

8) E-learning: The struggle never really ended. Down to looking for the darned textbook rental receipt. It would be embarrassing to admit how long I looked for it. However, it is amazing how much of the pile I thought it was in dwindled down to almost nothing as I hunted.

#paperssorted #filed #shred #recycle #neverfoundit #emailhadwhatineeded

9) Drive-by birthday parades: Yep, they are fun. Happy Birthday, Toni!

   #escapethehouse

10) Folded gift wrap: I don't even know if they still sell wrapping paper in folded sheets anymore, but what I found in my gift wrap box was perfect for tomorrow's four-year-old birthday boy!

    #hadthisforalongtime #doesntevensmellfunny

Here we go. Starting tomorrow, masks are now *required* in public. Let's flatten the curve. Wash your hands. We know the drill.

Day 41

May 1, 2020

Feeling punchy:

1) I took a 40-minute nap after dinner and woke up to the dishes being finished.

   #iwilltrythatagain

2) Refrigerate after opening: We will know tomorrow if that makes any difference or not. If Matt starts posting these daily shelter-in-place updates, it's because my husband and I are down and out. I'm joking. I hope.

   #carameltopping #inthecupboard
   #shouldberefrigerated

3) There was something different about today. The first thing I couldn't wait to do as soon as I got back home was take off my shoes.

   #notgotothebathroom

4) There's so much resistance talk about things going on now. Even the tulips in front of my house refuse to give in.

   #havebeendugup #yearsago #keepcomingback

5) My weekend goals include ordering an overdue baby shower gift because the shower was cancelled in March.

#coronavirus #julybaby

6) Just in case you are in the market for a birthday poster for a car parade, I have one you can use. It's even reversible.

#toni #jacob

7) The weather! I drove past a Kinder Care center and literally saw kids playing a running/chase game on their playground. That was the best sight all day.

*#letkidsplay #betogether
#wayitshouldbe #staffworemask*

8) I ordered groceries for tomorrow but selected "early ok" as my delivery option. My shopper reached out to me and told me he could get them tonight. You betcha, buddy!

*#earnedgrocerycredit #freegroceries
#titosandlemonadetonight*

9) Tonight's entertainment was another round of "5 Second Rule." Matt won again. Ok, we let some things slide. The scores were close: 20, 18, 15.

#goesfasterthatway #gameover

10) We're thinking about a big project while we shelter-in-place. I don't want a map of the world plastered on my Facebook page when

I ask if you have any recommendations for countertop work, so I will sneak it in here.

#bigprojectforus #seekingrecommedations
#facelift #commentbelow

I'm not sure what's in store for the month of May. The calendar is blank. It looks like a long, slow month ahead.

#yikes #followtherules

Day 42

May 2, 2020

Saturday stuff:

1) Cleaning: Traditionally, Saturday is known as a day for cleaning. I got right to it and cleaned my make-up brushes. Is it true that I put all that stuff on my eyes and face? Meanwhile, my son has been killing it with the vacuum cleaner in his room each week. Cue the Barney song: *Clean-up, clean-up, everybody do your share.*
#ilovebarney #bigpurpledinosaur

2) Masks: Form, function, and fashion. I went with fashion today and coordinated mine with the color of my shirt. A random woman in Meijer went with form and was wearing the whole plastic shield. I kept my manners about me and did not ask her if I could take her picture, although I wanted to. On the other hand, the guy at the local nursery went with function and cut the collar out of an old t-shirt and made it work as a mask. I had no problem asking him if I could take his pic-

ture. His original "mask" was the best I have seen yet!

#repurpose #noshameaskinghim #ackacknursery

3) Laundering masks: hand wash, hang dry . . . the new lingerie.

#thenewsexy

4) Discarded gloves in parking lots: This irks me to no end. Meijer should not have had to jimmy up a receptacle for such things, but they did. Go, Meijer!

#keepamericabeautiful #staysafe

5) Social distancing: Meijer is going hard on ensuring best practices are followed. Two of my favorite employees kept track of the number of people coming and going.

#storecapacity #newnormal #soweird

6) Giggle for the day: "If you are driving in your car with windows down wearing a mask . . . I'm certain you're the person who wears socks with open toe sandals."

#forthewin #cleverobservation

7) McDonald's: No one told me that my napkins would blow out of my car going 40 with both front windows down.

#isthatphysics? #notinhighschool #notincollege

8) Shelter-in-place reality: My monthly credit card bill for gasoline was only $83.00. It's usually $200.

#stayedhome #itmatters

9) Dinner prep: I baked a great piece of rainbow trout and green beans for 15 minutes at 400°. But I'm so reluctant to use my new baking sheet that my mother-in-law gave me for Christmas! I'm jealous when I see my Facebook friends' pictures of cookie dough on shiny pans and I think, "What's wrong with me? I don't have to use my ancient, crappy, dark pans . . . but there's nothing wrong with them." So, I get a gift and I don't want to use it.

#saving #whencompanycomes
#lifeistooshort #usethenewone

10) Envy: As I wrap up this post, I can hear a driveway gathering going on through the screen door. I can smell a fire in a fire pit.

#kumbaya #istherebeer #littlepig
#littlepig #letmein

Keep up what we are keeping up.

Day 43

May 3, 2020

Starting week #7: Shelter-in-Place

1) Reflection: I talked with my brother and sister-in-law tonight and we compared our lifestyles while sheltering-in-place. They are in Florida, a family of 4 at home. We are in Illinois with a family of 3 at home. Both of us are doing very well with abiding by the expectations, and quite frankly, pretty darn proud of us.

   #thisisus #attagirl

2) Sunday radio: They played "Jose Cuervo" for two weeks in a row and "You're the Reason God made Oklahoma" (David Frizell/Shelly West, 1981) was a bonus! My dad loved this song.

   #notachurchhymn #worksforaSundaymorningdrive

3) Masks and gloves: Nothing to see here, today, let's move along.

   #kids #mustwear #notfun

4) Whining: It seems everyone is fussing about how their hair is getting too long and shabby.

Honestly, I am enjoying watching my son's hair grow to see if it will be as wild and curly as his older brother's when he lets it go. As for me, I am starting to sparkle.

#howgraywoulditbe #notreallyablonde

5) Shelter-in-place activity this week: rounding up the ripped jeans, stained shirts, raggy underwear, and anything else that fits the "clothing drive" requirements scheduled for Saturday at Keep Northern Illinois Beautiful.

#cleanclothing #wearable #notwearable #allofit

6) COVID-19 beverages: It seems like one of the only things without restrictions is your choice of drink. Clearly, I can't drink lemonade and vodka. That goes down way too quickly. The frozen drinks are rather good. But anything in a red solo cup is good for me!

#odd #liquorstores #essential

7) Productivity: I am either 150% productive or 0%. So, after a little time on the patio with a frozen drink and slouching in a lawn chair, I had to come in and lay supine on the couch for another 45 minutes.

#freeagent #thenwashedwintercoats #guilt

8) Entertainment: Matt and I played 5-Second Rule tonight on Zoom with my brother's family in Florida. Technology is great, but oh, the set up to make the "studio" work is funny. We propped things up with boxes for

height to get the camera elevated and radios for weight to stabilize the box to prop the phone.

#whateverworks #homestudios
#iforgottowearlipstick

9) Kids: One of my kids moved to a new apartment this weekend, one is wondering what her next move is going to be, and one would probably like to "collect $200 for passing Go" for putting up with me day after day.

#shelterinplace #homesweethome

10) Should have: I should have washed the dinner dishes earlier tonight. I should have ordered that baby shower gift this weekend. I should have thrown my cloth masks in the wash with the winter coats. I cannot believe masks made this list after all today!

#theend

Here we go . . . another week . . . let's do it!

Day 44

May 4, 2020

Loose ends:

1) The longer this quarantine lasts the less productive I become.

   #notgood #needtoampup

2) The artwork I created in the piano dust last week is gone. Yes, I swished a dry cloth over it, and it disappeared.

   #magic #likeachalkboard

3) I think Charlie Beren's Facebook videos are funny and spot-on, especially "Dads During Tornadoes"

   #sirens #test #tomorrow #firsttues

4) The word has gotten out that I love jellybeans. Now I have a lot of them! One of my regular customers surprised me with a four-pound jar from Costco! I finally have a use for the stupid portion control bags I mistakenly grabbed at the store for the snack size bags.

   #ilovejacob #socialdistancelove

5) My daughter has entered the gig economy while she's in between her master's degree completion and her delayed start date for her career job. She is an on-demand grocery shopper for Shipt, the same company I work for.

#allinthefamily

6) Dinner was planned but the plan did not work out. The microwave is one of my best friends forever.

#notenoughleftovers #usedpulledporkinstead #fromthefreezer

7) Tomorrow is Cinco de Mayo and dinner is planned. One of our local restaurants, Fiesta Cancun, is on the menu. No cooking tomorrow night.

#grabacorona #notthevirus

8) They just don't make machines like they used to. I have two vacuum cleaners. One for the simple jobs and one for the real jobs.

#oldiebutgoodie #picturecrashed #shardseverywhere

9) I should take time to do the surveys after calls to investment companies.

#canijusttalktoaperson #please #justlikesocialsecuritycalls #promptafterpromptafterprompt #pleasepress1

10) Target.com is still open. It is 10 p.m. and I will order that baby shower gift tonight.

#goalmet #babydue #july

Day 45

May 5, 2020

Cinco de Mayo:

1) Radio: Luke Bryan's new song "One Margarita" (2020) came on and it sounds a lot like "99 Bottles of Beer on the Wall."

#history #repeatsitself #perfectsong #cincodemayo

2) Shelter-in-place for nonhumans: Insects seem to have taken up residence with us. My son told me there was a "cricket" (wasp) flying around in his bathroom this morning. The fly swatter and I took care of that bad boy right there on the spot. A moth and a gnat also thought they belonged here.

#tooearly #bugs

3) Masks: I spend about three to four hours a day in the grocery store doing Shipt orders. The last two days I noticed my upper jaw was feeling weird.

#mouthbreathing #toolong #mask

4) Art/design work: Some work looks too nice to be disturbed, so I didn't open a card from my little friend who gave me the jellybeans until the next day.

#dinosaurstickers #allover #thankyoucard

5) Working at home: Some days are just too hard and require a nap after work. Honest, we have paid our gas bill and we have heat, but a blanket makes a nap go so much better.

#husbandsnoozes #wearingahoodedsweatshirt #plusblankie

6) Eye roll: The eye roll from the guy in the car next to me is the universal language of things run amuck at curbside pick-up on Cinco de Mayo.

#everyoneiscelebrating #restaurantoverwhelmed

7) Food rationing: I think we are at the point that it's ok to use multiple eggs in cooking and not feel like they should be rationed.

#dessert #churrocreme #bruleebars #twodozenlimit #stillineffect

8) Shelter-in-place activity: "Doing my nails" with Color Street nail strips.

#imnotmadeformanicures #easyapplication #worthatry

9) Events: So many significant events, rites of passage, and milestones have been robbed by this virus. I am sorry for everyone who is missing those things or having them modified in such a way that it hardly resembles the

real thing. This would include my daughter's graduation for her master's degree.

#takepicturesanyway #celebrate #keepperspective

10) Test: Are there too many hashtags used in this post? Facebook will not recognize them if there are.

Day 46

Phases: Shelter-in-Place

Our governor has a 5-phase plan for Illinois. I want to be in Phase 5 three weeks ago, yet here we are. Another day in coronavirus land.

1) I'll start with masks. The craziest one and most original was a millennial wearing a hoodie backwards and pulling the hood up over his nose and mouth.

   #okthen

2) I saw a friend at the grocery store today. She had finished her shopping and was waiting for her friend/driver to finish her shopping. I am still disappointed in myself for not taking a few minutes to talk with her about her niece who died four weeks ago. The best we can do in the moment is to "say their name." I know her heart is broken in a million pieces.

   #slowdown #lifesisshort #ellen

3) Since I can't leisurely sip a soft drink because of wearing a mask, I try to schedule my pop break to go with my lunch, which I eat in my car. A Taco Bell gift card has been sit-

ting on the kitchen counter for the past two weeks (balance of $1.50), so I decided to use it today. As it goes, I couldn't find the silly thing when it came time to order, so now I still have it!

#nofunlids #nodietcoke #onlydietpepsi

4) Our dinner plan was mostaccioli and I even remembered to check to see if there was a leftover jar of spaghetti sauce in the refrigerator. Nope, not this time. But there are two different salsas open. And two grape jellies.

#topshelf #condiments #nothingmoldy

5) Tonight we listed the restaurants that we have ordered dinner from since we have been sheltering-in-place: Lino's, Oscar's, Smokey Bones, Lucha Cantina, Baci's, Hope and Anchor, and Mexico Classico. We have never used Door Dash or Grub Hub.

#hubbyisourdoordasher #donttellusaboutgrubhub

6) We dusted off the "Apples to Apples" board game for our evening entertainment. We have never played "Cards Against Humanity." We are still novices.

#wimps #wearenotcool #humanitycards
#notindemandanymore

7) Our spring work is ahead of schedule since there isn't anything to do. My husband almost has the pool filled and we had mulch delivered. Now we are the cool neighbors

who have a mountain of mulch in their driveway.

#eleventhousandsteps #hubbyspreadsmulch #pushthatwheelbarrow

8) The craziest thing I was asked to do today while shopping an order was to tell someone via text message what a certain perfume smelled like. Say, what? Honey, I get headaches from perfume so I couldn't tell you how they smell. They are all too strong for me.

#newinvention #sprayperfumeonphone #transmittopersononotherend #theydecide

9) My brothers and sisters must have observed a day of fast today. No one sent a picture of their dinner creations.

#idoubtanyonestarved #dinnerwasboring

10) I want to give a shout-out to my friend, Karla J. Clark. Her new book, *You Be Mommy*, is having great success. Congratulations, Karla!

#ilovelocalauthors #encouraging #amazon #barnesandnoble

Day 47

May 7, 2020

Is it just me?

1) I saw a round rusty cap in the grocery store parking lot and swore it was a doughnut. I even stooped to take a closer look and cocked my head to see the side of it. It had to be a doughnut! Who would leave a whole doughnut on the ground?! It was not a doughnut. I guess my mind was swayed by the $300 order I was delivering.

   #kidssnacksonorder #lotsofthem
   #doughnuts #notadoughnut #rustycap

2) I mailed cards out for Mother's Day. All five of them. I sent one to my mom, my mother-in-law, and three other people who are experiencing some extraordinary challenges right now as a mother.

   #hanginthere #youareloved

3) Shelter-in-place activity: "Tearing apart" closets and sorting clothes/textiles for the clothing drive on Saturday. Sometimes you just know you will never fit in some of your

favorite things again, and if you do, it will be so out of style you better not wear it.

#getridofit

4) Twenty-two texts later, my millennial kids have compared their Kitchen Aid mixers. That is so crazy! Who would think this is a coveted kitchen appliance at their age?

#whatintheworld #noneedforweddingregistry #butmaybeiwantonenow

5) A few new plants, a spread of mulch and a sunny day makes it look like summer has arrived. My former co-worker beat everyone to the May basket punch and dropped off a pansy long before that and it is now thriving in the flower bed.

#pleasenofrosttonight

6) This is a riddle: How many times do you have to drive through Taco Bell on the second day to spend the remaining $1.50 on a gift card? Answer: Two. Once to order and tell the guy you've got the card but can't find it and another time to drive back around because the card fell on the floor under your foot while you were messing with the hand sanitizer bottle.

#covid19

7) There's still a load of laundry to switch over and I am fading at the computer.

#winterhatsandgloves

8) I am working at 80% capacity tonight.

   #tootired #cantdoten

9) Number 10 intentionally left blank for you to hashtag.

   #humorme

10)

Day 48

May 8, 2020

Will this ever end? Shelter-in-place:

1) Overdue: We are all stalled and can't get things done or tended to because everything (mostly) is still closed. Things like haircuts, hair coloring, nails, appointments, practices, rehearsals, ceremonies, church, etc. I can live with the haircut/hair coloring thing being overdue, but it's time for me to get my goodie bag from the dental hygienist.

   #toothbrushbristles #fanningout #bettergotoCVS

2) Radio: I tire quickly of the commercials singing the praises of a local dentist on how he has changed someone's life, fixed their smile, etc. That is all good and well, but over and over and over and on one station after the other is too much. I switch as soon as it comes on until I find a station that is playing a song I like. Today's choice was "The Flame."

   #Cheaptrick #hometownband #nosiriusforme

3) Masks: I thought Matt would like to get out today, and he had a package to mail and

a donation to drop off. He grabbed a new mask and we "tried it out" in the car before he went in to mail his package. I had no idea we would be in this situation for this awfully long and need so many masks. One of my favorites (by standards of comfort) is a cloth one with elastic straps.

#function #fashion #stillnotnormal #doilookgoodwithcowsacrossmymouth

4) Closed: One of our errands was to stop at the postal station and the other was at the Boy Scout office. Well, gosh, the Boy Scout office was closed.

#duh #whatwasithinking #partofmelivesunderarock #boyscoutsarenotessential

5) Small business problems: When there's so much traffic for curbside take-out that it obstructs access for the adjoining business, the restaurant management does the right thing and sets up a route in the parking lot to redirect traffic so both businesses benefit.

#lovethyneighbor #beagoodneighbor #salamonesnorth #baskinrobbins

6) Small business appreciation: As I mentioned on Cinco de Mayo, there was some confusion and chaos at the restaurant where we ordered. My husband said they called today and apologized for the inconvenience and hoped we would come again.

#nocomp #stillnicegesture #everyyear #cincodemayodisaster

7) What my mom would do: If there would be an event happening in the neighborhood or at our house, she would take a picture. The tree they took down today was not in our yard, but I thought the hard work the guys were doing to lift the cuts into the truck was worthy of a picture.

#likemotherlikedaughter #nothingtodowithcovid19
#buttheydidgoodwork

8) Shelter-in-place happy hour: I had my own version of happy hour because my guys were busy with other things. I would like to think I really like Captain Morgan and Diet Coke, but it is just ok.

#mydadalwayssaid #cantgowrong
#withabeer #heisright

9) COVID-19 press conferences: I had hoped to spread out the time it took to run two errands with Matt so he could enjoy the outing, but when I suggested we get an ice coffee or something, he said, "No thanks, I want to get home to watch the press conference and then Ellen." Seriously. He said that. And he grasps quite a bit of it.

#currentevents #askmyson #knowsthename
#winnebagocountyhealthdept #administrator

10) Parades and reverse parades: The schools, administrators, teachers, PTOs, etc. are doing some cool things to stay connected to students and families.

#applause #applause #applause #bringbackschool

It is Mother's Day weekend. Good for some, hard for others. Make someone's day in some way.

Day 49

May 9, 2020

Lost list:

1) Truth be told, I make a list throughout the day to remember the things I want to recall while we are staying-at-home during this pandemic. Sometimes it is two lists on different scrap pieces of paper, like today. And some days, like today, I cannot find either of them.

   #shortlisttonight

2) Shelter-in-place activities today:

   a) Lined two more shelves and used up the last of the shelf liner. Make a note to buy more. No peeking . . . my shelves are a smorgasbord of different patterns of shelf liner.

   b) Checked balances on gift cards left from Christmas: Target $0.36. Macy's $46.30 . . . oh yeah, we returned those scarves and forgot about the credit. I am sure Macy's is having an online Mother's Day sale this weekend. I bet I can spend more than the balance!

c) Vacuumed but was incredibly careful not to suck up the throw rugs because gosh, I wouldn't want to have to go the extra step and shake them out, too!

d) Filed some valuable paperwork and added other documents to the paper shredding pile.

e) Listened intently to what my son has planned for us for Mother's Day tomorrow. Change of plans from going to the state park to watching a movie I have never heard of (*History Boys*).

#notmuchofanoverachiever #today

3) Virtual ceremonies: I have been able to see two of our friends' kids graduate from college today. It is great to watch but makes me sad that it happens in their living rooms.

#congratsallaround #watched
#whiledrivingthroughportillosrestaurant

4) Birthday cake: My giggle for the day was reading the meme about the birthday person blowing out the candles and all of us eating the cake after their breath and saliva was used to extinguish the flames.

#seemsnastynow

5) SIP DIY HH: That is code for Shelter-in-Place Do It Yourself Happy Hour. My friend found the frozen margarita mix, and more, at the grocery store where her husband couldn't find them.

#drink #chugalug

6) Shelter-in-place back in the day: I delivered an order today that was two houses down from our former home. It felt good to see it again and smell fresh grass being cut. We outgrew that home and moved to a ranch design in 2003. I was at "Lucy's house" today, but Lucy is long gone, too.

#romeavenue #greatneighbors

7) Mother's Day: We usually avoid the restaurants on Mother's Day, and I guess this year won't be any different because they're closed anyway. That didn't stop us from trying curbside tonight though, with limited success. One restaurant we tried had an extremely limited menu and was too far across town, two were going to close in 30 minutes, so we ended up at Portillo's.

#sortoflocal #wetried #italianbeef

8) I started this entry about the cost of sodas from the self-serve coolers at the checkout lanes but deleted it because it was so lame. And then I thought about all those Starbucks that are closed in the stores during the pandemic. The coffee drinkers are probably long past the Starbuck withdrawals by now.

#butsavingalotofmoney

9) This list is longer than I thought it would be.

#stretching #tofillitup

10) Ahh . . . .made it to 10. If we divided this list in half it would have symmetry.

#perfectworld #butnumbertwoissolong
#wouldntbesymmetrical

Another week is almost finished. Slow and steady wins the race.

Day 50

May 10, 2020

Observations on Mother's Day while shelter-in-place:

1) I won't gush, and I won't lament about Mother's Day. For some, it is a great day, for others it smarts. I am glad my mother is in my life and honored to be my kids' mother. I asked Matt, my middle child, if he could pick a different mother who it would be. Without flinching, he said I was ok.

   #phew #notrapforhim

2) The first song I heard on the country oldies this morning was "Delta Dawn." I *think* that was a song that one of my cousins sang long before karaoke was cool. Then I thought about my cousins whose mother died while they were so young. I have too many cousins to tag here but it gave me a moment to pause and think about that.

   #ralphskids #bettyskids #peteskids

3) My family knows I don't want or need lavish gifts on Mother's Day. But yeah, that gift card for McDonald's works simply fine!

   #tendietcokes #myvice

4) I called my mom and really enjoyed hearing about her 2.5-hour online euchre games with her hometown gal pals. She said it was just like she was back there having a card game with them.

#besties

5) The Stay Home order was in full effect here today. I cooked a simple dinner and thought to myself: carrots in the one-pound bags are worthless. Why bother peeling those pathetic things?

#nobulkcarrotsatthestore #bringonsummerharvest

6) At the same time, I wondered why there is a plastic shaker cap on the bay leaf bottle. Like you would be able to shake a bay leaf through one of these small holes?

#toomanysteps #togetonebayleaf

7) I stalked a friend's page after I saw his tweet on twitter. His profile picture shows him and his girlfriend enjoying beer flights. Now I am mad that this shelter-in-place is lasting so long. I want to go out for a beer flight.

#pleasereleaseus #beerathome #notthesame

8) I think it is kind of weird when people post their screen shots of their Zoom or Facetime calls. Yet, here we are, talking with my oldest son today and seeing his new apartment and his shelter-in-place wild hair.

#hegetsthefirstappointment #callthebarber

9) Be sure you know how much I appreciate your "likes," "loves," and "hahas" on these trivial matters I prattle on about each day. More importantly, your forgiveness on my typos, funny sentence structures, wrong verb tenses, etc., is humbling. When I go back and re-read some things I wrote, I just smdh. Mom, smdh means shaking my damn head.

#needaneditor #lateatnight

10) Thanks to my three kids for calling me "Mom" and not trading me in.

#iamahappymother

Day 51

Refrigerator clean-out:

If it was leftover in the refrigerator, I peeled, diced, chopped, mixed, and tossed out anything that "must go." What was revealed:

1) Zucchinis bought in the store are about 1/10 the size of those grown in Illinois and Iowa. They also shrivel very quickly and become squishy.

   #tossed

2) The yellow summer squash will be lucky to make one more day. It does not look like it's going to be worked in the menu tomorrow night but I'm saving it just in case.

   #nodoubtitwillbetossed
   #margheritapizza #tomorrownight

3) I was certain I was going to be a Tupperware lady at some point in my life. That never came to pass, but I do love (almost) all things Tupperware though! The onion keeper is amazing!

   #toyshapesorter #didnotlikethat
   #nowiamagroceryshopper

4) There was 1/2 of a lime that was still good (even though it was in a Ziploc and not Tupperware). I knew there was one ginger beer left on my recently reorganized fancy-dancy liquor shelf in the pantry. They pair perfectly well together.

   #moscowmule #fixdinner

5) The first watermelon of the season is never as good as it looks.

   #mushyparts #atesomeofit
   #tossedsomeofit #waitforsummer

6) Fixing dinner and cleaning up always takes way longer than it does to eat it. My son portrays a waiter and clears the table.

   #leavehimatip #stillmarvel
   #athisbalanceandwalking #braintumorsurvivor
   #cerebellumdamage

7) My whole day wasn't consumed with cleaning out the refrigerator. That only took about 30 minutes but is 60% of this list.

   #dicechopcutpeel

8) Since I spend about 4 – 5 hours a day at the grocery store, you quickly learn strategies to covet items that will be gone by the time you shop orders for later in the day.

   #hidethelysolspray #comebacklaterforit
   #stealthshopper

9) It's a good thing I have good reading skills because if I didn't, I could have mistaken

the Coors Light for the Diet Coke since they looked similar in the store display. Coke Zero helps you discriminate, as it was placed between the two similarly looking displays.

#strategicplacement #makegooddecisions

10) Shopping for others piques my interest to try things I've never heard of, like Ding Dong pudding.

#whoknew #yesiboughtit
#probablynotasgood #astherealthing

Day 52

May 12, 2020

Total slug:

The deeper we get into the quarantine/stay home mess, the more unproductive I become. *#mysadstateofaffairs*

1) I didn't take any pictures today.

   #nothingtriggeredme

2) Well, there was one incident that I would have loved to have taken a picture of but thought how rude that would have been. The cashier at the McDonald's drive-through was wearing a mask, under her mouth and over her chin. But she had the bands crisscrossed over her ears like they say is more effective for those who wear glasses, but yeah, otherwise totally ineffective.

   #trytryagain #reallymademelol #sipthedayaway

3) When I am not productive, my mind turns to mush. I haven't remembered to get hand soap for three days.

   #outofstock #anyway #barofsoapatsink
   #nowthatsoldschool

4) The lack of oomph has also resulted in not having a to-do list, so I picked up a book from my daughter's bookshelf that I started a short time ago. It's starting to get good, but I should request what I want to read from the library and use curbside service.

#wouldrequiremypassword
#toomuchwork #tolookitup

5) Leisure reading:

#prefer

#authorJodiPicoult

#pleasewriteanotherbook

6) I can cut myself some slack . . . I have made a few calls about our home improvement project. Who knew those types of businesses were considered essential?

#bringiton

7) The day was beautiful and worthy of shorts and a t-shirt when I got home, but I had to put on a hoodie soon after that.

#makeyourmindup

8) I use three news "sources" for information about the virus. The newspaper, the radio recap, and my son. Matt gives us an update and I am now aware that our part of the state is expected to stay in Phase 2 until May 29.

#becausehetoldme #ibelievehim
#cantcomesoonenough

9) Tomorrow will be an even more unproductive day. I won't even have to fix dinner.

#orderout #supportsmallbusiness

10) Maybe I will get a kick in the pants tomorrow with some inspirational vibe on my McDonald's pop lid.

#stepitup #giterdone #getoffyourlazybutt
#maketodaycount

I think there's truth in the saying of "keep on keeping on." Let's go.

Day 53

8:30 p.m.: Shelter-in-place

1) Children, it is 8:30 p.m. Do you know where your parents are?

   #readyforbed #toomanymidnights #turnintoapumpkin

2) To-do list: There were three things on it today; 66% accomplished.

   #buysoapcheck #readmondaypapercheck #gotobanktomorrow

3) Public Bathrooms: With no uncertainty, I probably use the grocery store's bathroom as often or more in one day's time as I do at home. Pausing to use the bathroom can be such an interruption in my time-sensitive job. (Just kidding). But today, the lady in one of the stalls must have waited till the very last possible moment to use the bathroom because the muffled sounds of relief coming from her were quite apparent!

   #aahhh #saveontoiletpaper #usestorebathroom #bathroomveryclean

4) Masks: A friend of mine bought herself a sewing machine, created her own pattern, and started making cool, fancy masks. We traded one Batman pillow for three masks.

#itsallabouttheelastic #savesonyourears

5) I am the broken link in the posts that ask you to post 10 pictures over 10 days of some theme, no questions asked, no explanation.

#sorrynotsorry #waytoomuchwork #forme
#butienjoyyours #doublestandard

6) Sending a shout-out to my friend as she takes some time off to potty train her son. She would like him to go to preschool this fall if Illinois opens by then!

#sendgoodvibes #Quentin #gladthosedaysareover

7) My husband said Wisconsin is going to be opening fairly soon. He and Matt will be one of the first to cross the state line to get in at Cost Cutters.

#haircuts #wisconsinbeer
#bringbackspottedcowbeer
#onlyavailableinwisconsin

8) I am dreading this summer for all the families who have kids that need activities and daycare. It sounds like the usual summer programs will be virtual. How do you play Dodge Ball on Zoom? Or make banana boats at Girl Scout camp without a campfire?

#sodisappointed #thisreallysucks

9) We all have funny friends, and then we have very funny friends, or even really funny brothers! But I can count on friends on Facebook for posting the funniest things almost every single day.

#thankyou #scrollfacebook #allday

10) I love the meme that says, "ripping off your mask when you get back in the car is the new taking off your bra when you get home."

#icanrelate #bigbustedwomen
#freethegirls #braasamask

My son loves to reference Wednesday as Hump Day. We're here folks, and almost through it. Keep flattening the curve.

Day 54

May 14, 2020

There may not be a list of 10 tonight.

I'll see what I can do, but I can always borrow and steal someone else's post from today if necessary.

#littlehelpfrommyfriends

1) Radio: My favorite song today was "Baby Love" (Supremes, 1964). As I was driving down the road my shoulders were bobbing up and down to the beat, first one and then the other. I bet if you play those words in your head, your shoulders are doing it, too.

#dareyou #ibetyoudidtoo

2) Belvidere, IL: For my out of state peeps, Belvidere is a town of about 25,000 people and 15 minutes from my home here in Rockford, IL. I moved there from college for my teaching job. It always feels like home when I am over there. There was an older gentleman standing in his yard, cap on, hands in his pocket and gave me a nod as I drove past. Just as if I were one of his neighbors at the end of the block.

#homesweethome #anotherplaceintime

3) Shelter-in-place: It seems some of you are making your outdoor spaces welcoming with flowers, cute lawn accessories, patio furniture, etc., while you shelter-in-place. As for me, I'm looking at a backyard pool that might need an act of a good scuba diver soon to find the leak/fix it or it will be a dry well.

#woeisme #keepingitgoing #forafewmoreyears #ihaveindoorgeraniums

4) Social distancing: It is always a win when I have my shopping cart going the right direction as to the way the arrows are pointing. If not, I turn my cart around, so it looks like I'm going the right way.

#soconfusing #worthwhileattarget #targetaislestoonarrowanyway

5) Masks/no mask: I decided to do a grocery order this evening and three guys (adult men) walked in without masks on. One guy's britches were hanging off his butt, so you get the picture.

#protesting #makeastatement #headtotoeviolations

6) Metric system: My son is a master at finding things to make/bake/cook that always include metric measurements. The struggle is real, even when I was going to cheat and use a seasoning packet for Shepherd's Pie tonight. Nope, there are metric measurements on the packet, too.

#cantwin #nevermasteredmetricsystem

7) As long as I am talking about food: If you see the Utz brand of potato chips in your store, don't buy them. They taste just like Ruffles and you will not be able to stop eating them.

#trustme #goesgreatwithdietcoke

8) Motivation: The home improvement project has gained some momentum and thankfully, it will not be a DIY. Now hurry up already and let's get this done.

#somethinggood #shelterinplace

9) If I have to resort to mentioning the weather, it shouldn't count as one of my Top 10 remarks. But if the rain could fill our pool . . .

#raindropskeepfallingonmyhead #burtbacharach

10) Note to self: Remember to use hand sanitizer.

#imslipping #havefourinthecar #whatsmyexcuse

Now that I have admitted I've been forgetting to use hand sanitizer, I own it. New resolve. I will do better tomorrow!

#ithinkican #ithinkican #ithinkican

Day 55

May 15, 2020

Graduation (should have been) Day:

1) It would have been a beautiful day for a graduation ceremony. It was beautiful, but no graduation ceremony. My daughter's cohort/department was having a Zoom ceremony/get together this afternoon, so at least there was some sort of a climactic end.

   #bacherlorsandmasters #universityofmissouri #columbia #mizzou

2) Carrie will be hanging out in Columbia, MO until her lease is up in mid-June. Her job in Springfield, IL is delayed until the restrictions are eased so I'm hoping she will be here at home for a few weeks this summer.

   #job #healthcareadmin

3) We had a family outing today. Woowee! We went to the counter-top company and that took all of 30 minutes.

   #bigday #liveditup #rolledthewindowsdown

4) Our "home office" is not anything you would see in Modern Living or House Beautiful. It's

more like Grandma's Attic with a ukulele laying across the printer, six boxes of cookbooks in front of the bookcase, a Mickey Mouse pad at the computer, and a drawing tacked to the bulletin board that my now 30-year-old nephew sketched in 2007.

#truestory #shouldbepurging #insteadofwriting

5) The cookbooks were inherited when our good friend and neighbor moved to Iowa a year ago. The plan was to have a used book fair. The date had to be changed a few times and COVID-19 has also affected it. I think next Saturday will be a free curbside cookbook giveaway.

#comeandgetthem

6) Someone mentioned on another friend's post that they keep forgetting their garbage day since their routines are all turned upside down. I have noticed we have more garbage and recycle materials than usual, but my husband is fastidious with the garbage schedule.

#wewillneverforget #sundaynights #countonit

7) Tuesday Trivia used to be a thing until everything was shut down. Now we do the Better Business Bureau Order Out/Dine-In Trivia game over Zoom and it's a good thing you can't see the three of us lined up on the couch. Because if you could, I would be yawning, Matt would be sitting at attention, and you

wouldn't think my husband cared one bit, but he and my son know all the answers.

#baratmosphereisbetter #needmusicandjive

8) Hearts flourish in windows all over town. It's an "all in this together" sort of thing. I loved seeing the windows in an upstairs of a commercial building today. I don't know if it's an apartment, a storage room full of junk, or what, but for a brief second at the stop sign, I breathed it in.

#somethingsaboutcovid #areok #ihearthearts

9) The coolest thing I saw on Facebook today was a friend and her husband having a date night. He lined up a progressive dinner by driving around to some of their favorite places and getting tastes from each place. First stop was McDonald's for Diet Coke.

#shesmykindofgirl #datenight #covidstyle

10) My good friend from high school just popped in with a comment on last night's list. She can't believe I'm still writing and able to come up with 10 things each day. Hahaha!

#neithercani #mynewnormal #covid19boredom

In case you are wondering, I used hand sanitizer several times in my car today. Over and out.

Day 56

May 16, 2020

Shelter-in-place. Still.

1) Social distancing: Target takes it literally when the doors open at 8 a.m. There isn't any clustering around the carts because everyone is lined up outside on the X's, six feet apart. They have people enter one by one.

#oneatatime #notevendiscountedtvs #stillaline #saturdaymorning

2) Pivot: This seems to be the new buzzword. Pivot your business, pivot your focus, pivot your energy. In other words: try something new.

#pivotisthenewchange #stayfresh

3) Radio: Nothing popped today until "Piano Man" came on as soon as I pulled back into the driveway.

#ofcourse #singmeasong #lovethatsong #billyjoel

4) Graduation: It was great to see a gal in her cap and gown in front of the Rockford University sign having her picture taken.

#keepingitreal #takethepictures

#eatthecake #youearnedit

5) Shelter-in-place: The pool is open. Woohoo! Now if we can just pretend it will be in perfect condition for the summer.

#whoamikidding #neverbeenopensosoon

6) Ding Dongs: Ha! The dessert I made from the delicious looking picture on the Jello box is finished. Summary: It does not taste anything like a Ding Dong. It takes too much work. You must use the beaters twice (so must be washed during the process). Beat the cream filling for six crazy minutes. Too many bowls. Messy. "Drizzle the chocolate" was more like "plop." Conclusion: Spend $3.50 and get the real thing.

#nodisheswiththerealthing #probablysamecalories

7) Jamaica on the Grill: Yes, please! I picked up the menu today and we are planning on it for Wednesday dinner.

#newbusiness #menunotonline
#buylocal #smelledsogood

8) Kitchen duty: Apparently that was my job today. Ding Dongs, Shrimp Po Boys, British Roast Vegetable Salad with Stilton.

#mysonsrecipes #skippedthestilton
#dontlikestilton #moredishes

9) Masks: The sign on the door at the local international grocery store read "no shirt, no shoes, no face coverings, do not enter."

#newreality #notfun #whowillenforce #safely

10) The crazy days are over. There's toilet paper and paper towels in the store every day. There's even Lysol/Clorox wipes available a few times a week. But those Ramen noodles!

#limit2eggs #limit2milk #limit2distilledwater #shiptshopperknowsall

I may have to focus my list from Shelter-In-Place to something else. This has gone on too long. We all know what a 6-foot distance looks like without having to stand on the square, it's not unusual to see everyone wearing a mask, people aren't scrambling as if the sky is falling anymore, and we have toilet paper. We are ready for more. *#bringiton*

Part Two

Parallels to the Pandemic

May 17 – June 29, 2020

Day 57

Parallels to the Pandemic

I am not sure I have convinced myself that this is a new title, but I'm trying it out, at least for today. We are moving beyond "shelter-in-place," but we still are far from our old "normal."

1) Automatic response: I wonder how many times I go into a room or closet and turn the light on, full knowing exactly where something is that I am retrieving.

    #evenindaylight #eveninthedark #leavethedamnlightoff

2) Automatic response #2: I plug in the curling iron before I get in the shower. I automatically do it even if it is going to pour rain all day and I will be in and out of the weather at least six times.

    #whatsthepoint #cantbeatmothernature

3) Flying ducks: One came out of nowhere this morning while turning at an intersection and hit my windshield. It scared the heck out of me. I couldn't tell if it was injured, dead, or flew away. I couldn't see anything

in my rear-view mirror. It made me think of the movie *Sully* and how traumatic that must have been.

#duckslikerain #idontlikeducksonmywindshield

4) Boredom: I have not been bored enough yet to put away the Easter stuff in the basement. But I might be bored enough to make cookies and use up the Christmas candy that was still in the back of the freezer.

#tiredofmovingitaround
#peanutbutterblossoms #needshortening

5) More cookies: The Quixotic Bakery is a rather new business in town that has surely been affected by the shutdown. But they are "pivoting" and offering curbside pick-up for the Warm Cookie Bake and 50% of sales will go to the Arc of Winnebago, Boone and Ogle Counties, a local resource center for persons with disabilities. $10 for a box of 4 warm chocolate chip cookies with dipping sauces—chocolate and caramel.

#ordering5boxes #whowillbelucky
#surprisedwithcookies

6) Ding Dongs part 2: I got the idea to buy the box of mix from my one of my friends, who had it on her grocery order that I shopped the other day. They made their mix today and it is a beauty.

#worthyofacontest #happyboys

7) Google search bar: Who knew the little square in the google search box was so amazing?

#googlelens #languagetranslator
#shopping #menus #etc

8) To do list: Some of the smallest tasks do not make the list and yet, day after day, week after week, month after month, they are still not finished. I think I am finally tired of looking at an envelope of old pictures from the bulletin board in my office from two years ago that has been sitting by the bookshelf forever!

#photobook #rightnexttoit #justdoit #afraid
#willleadtobiggerproject #pandemicfreetime

9) Masks: I could not go a whole day without mentioning something about masks. I am convinced the disposable blue (sometimes yellow) cloth ones that they wear in the hospitals are the best. They are the perfect size, easy-on, easy-off, and lightweight.

#eyesmatter #canseewiththese #theydontcreepup

10) Sunday shoppers: Folks, grocery shopping is not meant to be a party. Even if the whole family of seven comes along and they are going down the aisle the right way, it is an "oversized load" in the roadway.

#getoutofmyway #yieldtotraffic #pandemicnascar

So, this is an early post tonight. Don't tempt me, I might start a new list of 10.

Day 58

May 18, 2020

Monday all day: Parallels to the Pandemic

1) COVID-19: I woke up thinking it was Tuesday for some reason and I had a dream that my husband, sons, and daughter were all being tested for the coronavirus. My role in it was to tell them the right way to enter at the School of Medicine for the test. (I think the one-way aisles in the grocery store are getting to me!)

   #weirddream #testednegative

2) Avatars: The new craze is designing an avatar of yourself. Honestly, I liked the chubby thighs on one of my friend's avatar. Someone, of course, had to ask what information Facebook was gathering from this graphic.

   #spoilsport

3) Funniest and most accurate meme today: Shared by a teacher friend: So, in retrospect, in 2015, not a single person got the answer right to "Where do you see yourself five years from now?"

   #whowouldhavethought

4) Masks: I try not to gawk, stare, or even glance, but sometimes I just cannot help it. The most original and basic one today was a white terry cloth towel clipped together in the back with an oversized, giant plastic clothespin.

#whateverworks

5) Toilet paper: There's three options to use a bathroom at our place. In order of proximity to the one closest to the garage when coming home is the one in my daughter's bedroom, then the hallway (my son's bathroom), and then my bedroom. I learned today that my son's bathroom still has some of the "good" toilet paper compared to my daughter's bathroom. I'll make the extra effort and go to my son's when I come charging in the house.

#cottonnelleisbetter #thanthecheaperstuff

6) Newspaper article: Coronavirus Pandemic "Everyone Has a Story" (Rockford Register Star/Associated Press, 5/17/2020). Yep, it mentions those of you who are out there making cloth masks, sourdough bread, etc. Yup, baking bread is what is new again.

#breadtakesyeast #notme #yeastisnotmybff

7) Ketchup (off topic): There was a bottle of ketchup on one of my orders today that I had never seen. It gave me a flashback to when my mom made homemade ketchup.

#thatwasnasty

8) Rebel under quarantine: I was tempted to try cooking the frozen vegetables in the steamable bag for dinner tonight with the wrong side up in the microwave. Like, what would really happen if the instruction side were face down?

#getyourkicks #notthatgutsy
#noteboredenoughyettoseewhatwouldhappen

9) Family bonding time: We had another game of Apples to Apples tonight. The box says over 5 million games sold and it is the Party Box. That is funny. I have never played it at a party.

#mysonsfavorite #playedthreegames
#vocabularybuilder #historylessonsoncards

10) End of the list: I could probably add something else, but the program on the TV in the next room is driving me crazy.

#weirdshows #hubbylovesit #goodnightfromme

Day 59

I got nuttin'—Parallels to the Pandemic

It has been a slow day in my pandemic world. Just four little bits and then I will need your help for the rest.

1) Interesting read: A newspaper editorial was spot on: "The Rituals of 2020" (Kathleen Parker/Washington Post Writers Group/ Rockford Register Star, 5/19/20).

   #ceremoniesmatter

2) Masks: As quickly as I rip my mask off when I leave the store another person lights up a cigarette as she loads 4 cases of Diet Coke in her car.

   #somebadhabits #worsethanothers

3) Filler for the list: The flowers I got for Mother's Day are still genuinely nice.

   #thankyouson

4) Jellybeans: They are all gone save for a few black ones for my husband.

   #tillnexteaster #endoflistfortoday

5) That's it. Your turn.

6) Go ahead. It is fun.

7) You're up.
    #covid19 #ramblings

8) Ramblings: That could have been my new title.
    #nevertoolatetochange

9) Be my guest.
    #yourworld #covid19

10) Ready, set, go!
    #youareit

Day 60

May 20, 2020

I've got 10 (plus) tonight: Parallels to the Pandemic

I am sending a huge shout-out to all of you that helped me with my list of 10 last night. It was so fun to look at your COVID-19 world!

1) 60 Days: Shelter-in-Place, Stay Home, All in Together, Quarantine, COVID-19, Coronavirus, etc. Call it what you want, but 60 days long is a bit much.

   #overit

2) Travel/Vacations: There still seems to be a stall in planning for vacations or other travel at this point. Instead, I took the postcards off the refrigerator and lived vicariously through our trips last year.

   #nowinphotobook #postcardsmakebetterpictures #newyorkcity #sanfrancisco #bahamas #yesplease

3) Delivery services: I arrived at a home today at the same time as a Fed Ex driver. She had 110 deliveries today. I had six Shipt grocery deliveries. Crazy!

   #canyouimagine #peopleordereverything

4) Hand sanitizer: Is it weird that I have a favorite hand sanitizer in the car?

#yesthatsweird #handiwipestoo

5) Masks: A lady had a black and white checked shirt on today and a black and white checked mask. Seriously? Is this what it has come to? Matching masks with your daily wear?

#wholenewlevel #youvegottobekidding

6) Haircuts: The sweetest 88-year-old lady told me today that she needed a haircut so badly and was wishing the salons would open. I asked to see what her hair was like in the back.

#aponytail #aboutthreeincheslong #godblessher

7) Organizational support during the pandemic: I bought Girl Scout cookies from a friend who is a Girl Scout leader. The Scouts couldn't have their cookie sales at stores, etc., this year so they have leftovers. Let her know what you want, and she will hook you up. No contact payment, no contact delivery.

#venmo #paypal #thinmints #tagalongs #trefoils #allkinds #mysonatehalftheboxoftrefoils

8) Dinner: Jamaica on the Grill take-out: So good! It's best if you call for their daily menu. They have two options per day during the pandemic. Call first, call early. We got the last four dinners at 5:15 p.m.

#jerkchicken #macncheese #cabbage #candiedyams #redbeansandrice

9) Radio: "All to Myself" (Dan + Shay, 2018). They sing about being "jealous of the blue jeans that you're wearing and the way they hold you so tight." Dude! You think that is comfortable??!

#thinkagain

10) True confession: Some days I just need two Diet Cokes from McDonald's. Like today.

#nogriefplease #feelingbubbly #sipforjoy
#mamasaid #therebedayslikethis

11) What friends said: I love your lists and hashtags from yesterday.

#hashtagisafunnyword

Day 61

May 21, 2020

Living the (mundane) dream: Parallels to the Pandemic

It has been just another day in pandemic paradise. Nothing that made the earth shake, except . . .

1) Hashtags: A bumper sticker, probably called a "cling" now or something like that, said "this # is a sharp, not a hash tag." Even though I am not musically inclined, I got it right away!

   #itsreallytictactoe

2) University of Northern Iowa buddies: My Facebook feed said it was one of our friend's birthday today. Another friend bet it would make my Top 10 List. One of our friends wished "Tooey" a Happy Birthday. No one called him Dave. So, Happy Birthday, Tooey!

   #missyouguys #UNI81

3) Other birthdays today: My dear-old-dad would have been 88. Plus, shout outs to Kathy, Mari, and Bianca!

   #cheers

4) Unscheduled time: The pandemic gives one the freedom to use time almost any way you want. So, I made a margherita pizza at 3:00 in the afternoon with the leftover mozzarella, tomatoes, and basil.

   #ilovebasil #dinner #fouroclock #livingontheedge

5) Masks: It is impressive when you don't see someone very often but can still recognize them even when they're covered with a mask. Hi, Eric!

   #itwasthebeard #gavehimaway

6) Edited—changed my mind.

7) Edited—changed my mind.

8) Edited—changed my mind.

9) Cookies: One more commercial break for supporting organizations during this time. Quixotic Bakery's cookie sale supporting the Arc: Check out the Cookies and Compassion event on Facebook.

   #beacookiemonster

10) So, a pretty ordinary, mundane day today.

   #keepthefaith

Day 62

May 22, 2020

Another week down: Parallels to the Pandemic

It's Friday and this wraps up another traditional work week. I am quite sure I started counting the stay-at-home quarantine days on the Monday of the first week that things were officially shut down. On the other hand, my son listens to the governor's conference each day and works from a different number. Either way, it has been a long time.

1) Shock: The blast of cold water coming from the shower head is enough to shock your system at 6 a.m. I was not the one who forgot to turn the toggle on the shower head to the hand sprayer when finished.

   #yowwww #playingvictim

2) Finders/Keepers: The day improved significantly when I found $15.00 in the back pocket of my jeans.

   #launderedmoney

3) Clorox wipes: I am still trying to figure out why people have been so determined to get Clorox or Lysol wipes. Whatever happened to using a bleach water solution: 1-part

bleach to 10 parts of water? As far back as I can remember, preschools and day cares have been sanitizing their toys and surfaces forever with this solution.

#pleaseexplain #lemonbleach
#lavendarbleach #bleachischeapertoo

4) Masks: College football returned in 1918 at Georgia Tech during a pandemic. They wore masks to the game.

#historyrepeats #bringbacksports
#bringbackeverything

5) Win: Neither of the other two cars in the first drive-through lane knew we were competing when I drove up to the empty lane.

#mcdonalds #outsidelane #alwaysgoesfirst
#iwin #highlightofmyday #timetosipaway

6) Edited post from last night: I deleted #6, 7, and 8 after I posted last night. I had some things there, but it did not settle with me. Some of you saw it, some of you thought I wimped out. Ha! Fooled you!

#nodoovers #onechance #eachday
#wasntsure #ihadmyfactsstraight

7) Hair salons: We all know what that jar of blue stuff is that sits on the counter at the hair salon/barber shop. They have always had it and used it. But apparently some new training was required for the cosmetologists

before they can reopen. Really? Seems absurd but thank you for the compliance!

#barbicide #butareyourscissorssharp

8) Partnerships: It's great when businesses create ways that are mutually beneficial for them and a local social service agency, especially during these "unprecedented times." Fresh, warm chocolate chip cookies (from Quixotic Bakery) wrapped up this "all in together" kind of night.

#pivot #doordrop #sharethegoods #cookiemonster

9) Graduation Day: What would have been graduation day for one of our local high schools was instead a day of individual family celebrations. The 2020 graduates did not get the fun of continuing a long-standing tradition of spraying silly string after the ceremony or lighting up cigars outdoors. But life goes on and school is done.

#congrats

10) Memorial Day and the pandemic: My radio crush says honor the holiday even though there will not be parades, festivals, and picnics. Wear red, white and blue, decorate a grave, fly the flag. Our flags are up!

#arlingtoncemetary #eternalflame #somoving #landofthefree #homeofthebrave

Have a good weekend everyone. By this time next week, we should be starting to see a new light!

#cantwait

Day 63

May 23, 2020

Starting the day backwards: Parallels to the Pandemic

I took the 3rd grade mantra "read 20 minutes every day" to the max today, so my list starts at the end of the day and back tracks to the beginning.

1) Reading: I finally finished a book that got really good about half-way through (just like the last one I read!). But I did spend some time looking for it for a while.

   #lost #foundinmakeupdrawer

2) Supporting local business: When the tornado sirens rang for the second time this afternoon, we chucked the plan for grilling. Instead, we ordered dinner from Tom and Jerry's, a local sandwich shop. I had the best gyro salad ever! Get your Greek on!

   #opa #bringtheouzo

3) Tornadoes: We were spared by the bad weather and blessed with a rainbow. Rainbows make the list of the Top 10 things everyone posts when they see one . . . just

like sharing that the sirens are blaring, as if we didn't know.

#everyonelovesarainbow #cuejudygarland

4) Pandemic free time: Makes you feel guilty if you do not do something productive to balance the loafing around time.

#scrubbedkitchenfloor #readgoodbook

5) Holiday gift guide: If anyone still needs the December 2019 Holiday Gift Guide from the Chicago Tribune, I can pull it out of my recycle pile before Tuesday.

#goodidea #atthetime
#undercoffeetableallthiswhile

6) McDonald's: Now there is a person standing outside the drive through window to hand you your order. What is up with that?

#PPE #haveacokeandasmile
#1979commercial #doyouremember

7) Entertainment: My son has been entertaining us with live music from his room.

#singing #circleoflife #playingbugle
#shelterinplace

8) Small business: A showroom does not have to be fancy to sell a good service or product. Good, hardworking people can do that, too.

#essentialbusinesses #manyareclosed #covid19

9) Small thoughts: Have you ever wondered if anyone saw you put an item at a store on a

random shelf when you decided you didn't want it rather than taking it back to its right place? No?

#meeither #iwouldneverdothat

10) True confession: I would still prefer a thick, old-fashioned yellow pages book to look up businesses who do counter tops. The big companies are obvious, but what about the little guys?

#googleisonething #paperisanother
#canmakenotesintheyellowpages
#times #havechanged

Day 64

May 24, 2020

Things that are red, white, and cool: Parallels to the Pandemic

1) Candy at Meijer including Freedom Gummi Bears and Gummi Military Heroes.

   #godblessamerica #becarefulwithdentalwork #fillingsandcrowns

2) Red, white, and blue M&M's. I ate six and stopped.

   #impressive

3) Flags lining the Miracle Mile on State Street in my hometown.

   #beyourownparade #honorthosewhohavesacrificed #honorthosewhohaveserved

4) One last drink on my McDonald's gift card from Mother's Day.

   #reload #refresh #aaahsotasty

5) First dip of the season in the pool.

   #colderthanitlooks

6) Thoughts of having regular, open pool days again this summer since all other events, music and festivals are cancelled.

#covid19

7) Plastic wine glasses and koozies for poolside beverages.

#keepingitclassy

8) Fresh lemon slices in water.

#itsdefinitelysummer

9) Smells of lilac bushes wafting through the windows in my son's room and driving down neighborhood streets.

#tooshortlived

10) Creating a COVID-19 mask photo album from my camera roll.

#history #iwasbored #whilewaitingforsomeone

Enjoy the holiday. Groups of 10 or less. Social distancing. It is getting harder. Hang on.

Day 65

May 25, 2020

Memorial Day 2020: Parallels to the Pandemic

Touchpoints: Not the high frequency spots that everyone touches in stores, but what we have "touched" (seen) today.

1) My father-in-law's grave in Chicago, IL. United States Navy, 1944 – 1945. Pacific, World War II.

   #rogerwhite

2) My mother-in-law. She married my father-in-law in 1953 and had five kids.

   #bestmotherinlaw #hubbycookedforhertonight

3) My husband. United States Navy, 1975 – 1979. S.S. Barry (Mayport, Florida to Europe).

   #gibill #paidforcollege

4) My mom. She was the girlfriend of my dad while he was serving stateside in the United States Army, 1953 – 1954 (Fort Sill, OK) during the Korean War.

   #socialdistancetoday #outdoorvisit

5) Flowers for my mom. She always had lilacs and peonies in vases when we were kids. I brought her some lilacs, hoping they would survive the heat in a jar of water during transport.

   #suckedupwater #slightlywilted

6) My boys. We met my older son, Joe, between here and Chicago and called five restaurants before we found one that was open for curbside service. Two parks later, we found a picnic table in the hot sun.

   #sonneedshaircut #dontneedsunontheirfairskin

7) Birthday parades: So glad to get invited to these COVID-19 birthday celebrations and sorry we cannot make them all.

   #needmoreposters #makemoresigns

8) Goats and Cokes? Have you seen the photo of a baby goat in the front seat of a car sipping a McDonald's cup? Thanks for the laugh! But not in my car!

   #notmymcdonalds

9) Facts: Do you think I really knew all this stuff about the service men in my family?

   #ohhellno #askedmyhusband #twentyquestions

10) How long will these crazy lists go on? 'Til Day 100 or the end of wearing masks; whichever comes first.

    #dontgroansoloudly

Have a good week. Wearing a mask is normal. That is so weird.

Day 66

May 26, 2020

Summer came with Memorial Day: Parallels to the Pandemic

It is not copping out when I start talking about the weather. It is a fact. Summer has arrived and it was hot today.

1) May 25: Yesterday was seven months until Christmas. I would like to peer in a crystal ball to see how we will be doing by then.

   #fortuneteller #covid19

2) Flowers are in bloom: The peony bush I saw today was amazing. The owner of the home said it is 15 years old.

   #growoldgracefully

3) Weeds are in bloom, too: When the yard bag is full, take a break by the pool and admire the view.

   #doesntgetmuchbetter

4) Gym shorts: Gym shorts without pockets are worthless. Where do you put your phone when working in the yard?

#notabrastuffer #alwaysoncall
#Shipt #needmyphonewithme

5) Spiderworts: They are pretty when they bloom, but they are a pain in the bum.

#spreadtoomuch #hardtodigup
#crowdingmydaisies #bullies

6) The fun is long over: I bought my first sailboard when I quit teaching. Then my husband bought one before we were married, and I bought a new one. Our first child came along on our 1st wedding anniversary and that pretty much wrapped up our windsurfing days. I went out to the state park a few years ago and this old lady could still do it. It wasn't easy, or pretty, and I struggled, but it was fun to do it again. I rigged the board and tried it in our pool before we went out to the park. That was kind of crazy! Staring at those two boards in the garage has gone on long enough. Time to sell.

#somuchfun #icanteachyou
#greatcondition #rockcut #lakewingra
#neverdidlakemichigan #scaredycat

7) Car wash: Everyone must have gotten their car washed over the weekend. No line, but no vacuum cleaner either.

#touchpoint #thisismakingmecrazy
#vacuumedathome

8) Masks: My source came through tonight with a mask for my son, Joe. He tried a DIY and it has worked for the time being but enter the return to society and he needs to kick it up a notch, or at least I think he does.

#motherhen #wontknow #ifhewearsornot

9) Take-out dinner: I am not sure why I ask my guys where we should order dinner this week because I already have a restaurant in mind.

#collaborate #pivot #notalwaysaboutme

10) Recycle and shred: You'd think there wouldn't be a single sheet of paper left in this house with all the purging that's gone on these last nine weeks. Yet, there is one thing I am looking for and cannot find it.

#notessential #butitbugsme #quest
#ithasbeeninsameplace #forever #nowitsnot

11) Memorial Day Top 10: It was fun to share how well my mom is doing. I know she misses many things about Dyersville, her friends, her sisters, and brother, but she is content in her apartment out here by us. She has an apartment with a small deck, and she enjoys that very much.

#mysistersandbrother #livenearher

The season has changed. We need to rotate my son's clothes tonight. G2G.

Day 67

Wednesday: Parallels to the Pandemic

In a blink of an eye the day is over, and I realized I didn't make any notes so I'm winging it tonight. That is ok, because there's always things that make me laugh and see how different each day is from "normal" times, starting with masks! (There is always something about masks!)

1) Masks: We can now consider masks a fashion accessory. When they have their own rack at the store, it is official.

   #justlikeanecklace #orpurse

2) Mask meme: When I see someone wearing a mask below their nose, I just cannot "unsee" the meme that compares that image of the nose sticking out below the mask to someone wearing underwear down low and their "thingy" hanging out.

   #gladtheydontknowwhatiamthinking
   #gladtheydontknowwhatiamseeing

3) Our local park district: I brag on our park district a lot. That's because they are fabulous, and I will brag again for their creative planning during COVID-19. They are

bringing the summer program to their participants with hands-on activities/video instruction and virtual experiences.

#curbside #craftkittogo
#shelterinplace #socialdistance

4) Supporting small business: Dinner tonight was from a long-standing local. If you order Chinese food a few times a year, it is possible you will never have to buy a bottle of soy sauce again.

#soysaucepackets #chineserestaurants
#musthinkwedrinkthestuff

5) Shopping carts with drink holders: Rarely do you see shoppers strolling stores anymore with a Starbucks or Dunkin coffee (or McDonald's) cup in their cart. I think it is inappropriate to eat or drink something while wearing a mask. The only reason my cup was in my cart today was because it was too hot to leave it in the car while I shopped.

#dontbethatperson #maskshaverules
#lid #dontwastethetaste

6) Highlight of my day: Buying new garden gloves, spray paint, and throwing out old garden gloves.

#project #intheworks #nomoredirtyfingernails

7) Miracle: The flowers I bought today were planted today. That never happens!

#beattherain #evenfedtheimpatiens

8) Haircuts: Who would have thought this is one thing many people missed the most during this period of shutdown?

    #may29 #openforbusiness

9) Weather: Yes, I have run out of things to write. But to answer a question on a friend's Facebook post a few days ago, "yes, we are running the air conditioning now."

    #grateful #empathy #forthosewithout

10) Contest: I am challenging myself to limit *#hashtags* and see if they make the cut before Facebook does not boldface them.

(Have you seen the meme on face masks under the nose compared to a guy's "down there"? No. Just no.)

Day 68

Top 10 Thursday observations: Parallels to the Pandemic
Nothing today really relates to COVID-19, but that's ok.
We need a normal day.

1) Dry shampoo: Whoever thought this up? It makes your hair sticky and snarly.

   #shampoo #madeforwethair

2) Tostitos: What's the point of eating Tostito Scoops without salsa or con queso?

   #thentheyarejustchips

3) The bakery kid: There's nothing like making my day when the young kid in the bakery department said his day isn't complete until he sees me.

   #james #egoboost

4) Brain Tumor Awareness Month: It has been a really, tough couple of months for "kids" we know who have had brain tumors. A few have been/are in critical care and two have died. They weren't even in treatment

anymore. They were called survivors. Like all cancers, it knows no season, age, or gender.

#nondiscriminatory #devastating #wearefullyaware

5) Retired: I still cannot believe I don't have to get up and go to "work" every day. It has only been about two years since I retired, but gosh, this is great!

#retirementjob #isnotlikework

6) Cleaning: Mr. Clean, Fabuloso, and Pine-sol have distinct smells or associations for me. I'm ready for a new product.

#pinesol #girlscoutlatrines #cleaningbathroomstonight

7) Car wash: It will rain the next day or the following day if you wash your car, won't it? But my Toyota service gives you a coupon for a free car wash.

#nextsunnyday #lovetoyota

8) Crazy vegetable shapes: Every now and then there are the weirdest shapes in various veggies. I can't post the picture of one of the carrots today, because, you know, this is a G-rated page. But use your imagination. My customer called it "produce porn" and added it to her order for a gag gift.

#carrots #phalliclooking #peacesign

9) Cookbooks: The six boxes in front of my bookcase are going out on tables this

weekend so the walkers in my neighborhood can help themselves.

#comeonover #havesomegoodones #free

10) Masks: Ok, just one mention. I saw the craziest one yet. It wasn't even a mask. It was a cloth hanging off the guy's nose or attached to his glasses somehow. I don't know how it stayed on. I had to go in the next aisle because I was laughing so hard.

#masks #facecoverings #creativeorlazy

Tomorrow is Friday and start of the weekend. Phase 3 starts here in Illinois. Giddy-up.

Day 69

May 29, 2020

Phase 3: Parallels to the Pandemic

Today marks the first day of Phase 3, meaning some places of business have been able to reopen with limitations.

1) Barbershops are one type of business that reopened today. We drove past the place where my husband goes, but he figured they were just cleaning today.

   #needsahaircut #nbd

2) There weren't any bells or whistles that sounded today at our place to celebrate the start of Phase 3. In fact, today was just like any of the previous 68 days.

   #plainjane #nbd

3) NBD: Mom, NBD means no big deal.

   #language #interpreter

4) My son is our news anchor here in the house. Matt is on top of the current and local news regarding the reopening of businesses and services.

   #churchonsunday #localbrewery #outdoordining

5) The most original and most jimmy-rigged award for "no-contact" service goes to our main post office.

#clearshowercurtains #hungasbarrier

6) Some things in life are still free. Like the books that will be out in my yard tomorrow (Saturday) from 1 to 3 p.m.

#free #tellyourfriends #cookbooks #Tolkien #Tolstoy #romance #somekids

7) I did not intend to have a campfire on the kitchen stove while I was fixing dinner tonight, but it sure smelled like I did!

#woodenspoonburning #dontstartkitchenfires #eatout #instead

8) Gigi's Playhouse: Our Down Syndrome Achievement Center sadly missed a few of their major fundraisers during the quarantine shutdown. They could use your help.

#donationswillhelp

8801 N. 2nd St., Machesney Park, IL 61115

9) My little friend who was diagnosed with severe aplastic anemia is +158 days post bone marrow transplant.

#nowthatssomegoodnews #hair #comingin #birthdayparade #saturday #7yo

10) As always, it is a great day to be alive.

#covid19 or #nocovid19

Good night!

Day 70

May 30, 2020

This page intentionally left blank: Parallels to the Pandemic

1) We are struggling. Not as a family, but as a community, as a city, as a state and as a country.

   #notaboutcovid19 #nottoday

2) It does not seem right or kind to prattle on about trivial things that I experience today considering all that happened in our society over these past few days.

3) By ignoring the real issue of these incidents is making light of the fact that we have so much work to do in our country, health care issues aside.

4) While concerns around opening the economy are certainly legitimate due to the past two months of shelter-in-place, I must take pause and acknowledge that the recent days have taken a huge toll on us. We can all do better and do more.

5) Therefore, this page is intentionally left blank today.

   #georgefloyd

Day 71

May 31, 2020

Horrible: Parallels to the Pandemic

The events across the country are horrible. Totally devastating.

Pray for peace, healing, understanding, compassion, and everything else that is heavy on your heart.

Another day on whether I share a Top 10 list will not make a difference in stopping the violence, aggressions, and oppression we are witnessing or have historically experienced. Yet, I need another day to acknowledge the pain our communities and country are feeling.

Peace to you and yours.

Day 72

Let's go with it: Parallels to the Pandemic

For a few quiet moments, let's just take a break and allow ourselves this time to rest and refresh. I have a sangria next to me. Grab your wine, your beer, your coffee, or for you diehards, your water bottle, and savor five solitary minutes of unimportant news.

1) Drive-by birthday parades: One thing leads to another. When one of the birthday parades is a stone's throw away from the Wisconsin border, you pop into Beloit to get some Spotted Cow.

   #andkidkolsch #cheesecurds #wheninwisconsin

2) DIY presents: It's been a long time since I've been invited to a seven-year-old's birthday party, so I had to think hard on what little girls like. I came up with a DIY baking activity to make—Teddy-at-the-Beach cupcakes. The gift bag was packed with almost everything they needed to make the treat.

   #excepteggs #exceptoil #giftwrap
   #recylceribbonfromboutique

3) Sunday Funday: Matt noticed the flags were flying at the mini-putt golf course today, so we went for a round. Oh, goodness! It is a good thing we don't keep score.

#placesareopeningup #lilacswereheavenly

4) Dinner menu: Because I am a team player (yeah, right), I usually ask for suggestions for the week's plan. And then I am sorry.

#ratatouille #wednesdaynight

5) Masks: It is good to wash your cloth masks occasionally, right? Even after my husband has the laundry finished! If you throw a blanket in with it, you have a laundry load.

#hementionsiamspoiled #hedoesthewash
#imentionhegetsdinnereverynight #fairtrade

6) Double meaning: The slang phrase "stay in your lane" has generally meant take care of your own business and don't mind anyone else's. Now it can also mean "make sure your grocery cart is going the right way."

#myob #myogc #mindyourowngrocerycart
#aislearrows #notevenblackfriday

7) Other language I keep hearing: You do you and I do me.

#soundssnarky #bekind
#berespectful #especiallynow

8) Cookies: How can 20 cookies be too many over a package of 12? The customer did not want to sub the larger package.

#omg #freezetheextra
#nevertoomanycookies #ourplace

9) Anniversary: Today is the 1st anniversary of three of my son Joe's friends who have been ordained as priests.

#honortowitness #ordination

10) Rest: Five minutes are up. Time to get busy.

#youdoyou #idome #ijusthadtouseit #justforfun

Day 73

June 2, 2020

Reality vs Ordinary: Parallels to the Pandemic

We have separate issues going on right now. The pandemic isn't entirely quiet, but it's definitely in the back seat during these past days. It is hard not to be preoccupied with the protests and the core issues. The "risk" factor during these past few days is quite different, in a much more dangerous way. That is our reality right now, but the ordinary helps keep me grounded. So, let's get started:

1) Colon: No, not that kind. The punctuation kind. Have you noticed that on a computer keyboard it is to the right and on a phone keyboard it's to the left?

   #getsoconfused #wastedtime
   #lookingforitoncomputer

2) News overload: Help! I am drowning! I so desperately want to read articles in the Chicago Tribune, but they are so long. The local papers are a faster read, but I am still behind. The quickest news comes through Facebook, but that is not always verified or accurate. I had to give in and use some of last

week's unread papers and use them as a drop cloth, so the grass didn't get spray painted.

#papers #goodforsomething

3) History: So much has happened and changed these past 4 months. My niece said kids studying American history in years to come will need a whole semester to cover 2020. The vocabulary/key terms that would be highlighted at the bottom of the pages if they were still using books would be

#socialdistancing #masks #toiletpaper #shelterinplace #georgefloyd #riots

4) Toilet paper ratio: I would say the necessary amount of "crappy stuff" to "good stuff" is about 3:1. You need about 3 times as much crappy stuff to get the job done as you do good stuff.

#storesarestocked #panicisover #ihope

5) New BFF: Spray paint! I have four colors with a plan in mind to update some yard things, but I had to get it out of my system tonight. What was white is now purple!

#cruddylawnchair #didnotknow #spraypaintissomuchfun

6) Skin care: We've been preaching hand washing or to use sanitizer for the past 2.5 months. We need to keep that up. Now we must add sunscreen to our sermon.

#lipbalmtoo #hydrate #summerishere

7) Graduation Day: Apparently it was the official graduation day for some of our schools, even though there were not actual ceremonies. I saw a girl in the store with her gown on and several pictures on Facebook.

#dontforgethesekids #sendmoneyanyway #partyornoparty

8) Time: It is 10:30 and I am fading at the computer. I wonder what was on the 10:00 news? My friend gave me a quick overview of the marching protesters that passed near her house. My prayer tonight is to keep everyone safe. Oh, wait, that has been our prayer for the past 2.5 months already.

#keepitup #blackouttuesday

9) Final chapter of today's entry: #9 is up for your contribution.

10) Epilogue of today's entry: Good night.

Day 74

React, resume, and relax: Parallels to the Pandemic

1) React: Many people are taking stock of their principles and values, stepping out or stepping in to new or unfamiliar experiences and relationships. It is hard and necessary work.

   #bethechange

2) Resume: It has been long enough with wearing masks and not wearing lipstick. So, today I put lipstick on after my makeup.

   #itslikeputtinginthatlastpuzzlepiece
   #makesitcomplete #makeitalipstickday

3) Relax: There's no place like home, especially when there is a cool drink to go with it.

   #summerbeverages

4) Radio: There's always that one song that you just must sing along! That "Brand New Key" song by Melanie (1971) is such a weird song, but so much fun to sing!

   #rollerskates #turnitup #sing #youwillfeelbetter

5) Sneaky hint: Occasionally, there is a ghost in my house that has placed something on my bedside table as a reminder to do something.

#lionsclub #rosedayorderform #delivernextmonth

6) Good neighbor: One neighbor was helping another neighbor catch her dog when I came home tonight with mulch, flowers, and potting soil. I wonder if they noticed that I did not help.

#carryingmulch #conscienceisbotheringmenow

7) Resume: I am looking forward to the time when stores and restaurants operate on their regular schedule with full inventory.

#hurryupandshop #gardencenterclosesearly #safety #riots

8) Feeding time: Two baby birds were eagerly waiting for mama robin to come and feed them this afternoon. While we were outside on the patio, she didn't come back.

#hungrybabies #crowds #neverstopmefromeating

9) Feeding time for humans: Ratatouille was on our menu tonight, but the store was out of zucchini and summer squash.

#saveforanotherday #mediterraneantilapia #instead

10) Masks: Everything's better with bacon. I saw a picture of bacon strips cooked in rows

together with a looped strip on each side to look like a mask. Hilarious!

#photocreditrobertmoreau #dontknowhim
#butitisfunny #mmmbacon

As far as I know, it has been a quiet day in town, as you can probably tell by this boring list.

#boringisok

Day 75

Carry on: Parallels to the Pandemic

It was on a whim that I tapped out a list of how things were different on our first day of shelter- in-place. I thought it would be fun to keep track of how the coronavirus was affecting us and how we would handle the social isolation. I thought it might be a few weeks, but here we are 75 days later.

While the concern of COVID-19 is still very great, we are wrestling with civil/society problems in a much different way. I am struggling with continuing to share my daily antics during this sensitive time in our history. I am not ignoring the events in my community, our region, or our country, but I most likely won't use this space for those reactions. I am good with that. Let's carry on.

1) Pool time: The clock on the wall opposite the lounge chairs ticks away to strike a balance between loafing and getting something done.

#relax #swim #work #gethot #swim #repeat

2) Hints from Heloise: Yeah, that was a column a long, long time ago! Was it from Heloise that I got the idea to air our pillows and use

a little lemon spritzer to freshen them up? Or did I make that up?

#madeitup

3) Radio: "It's Five O'Clock Somewhere" (Jimmy Buffet/Alan Jackson, 2003) came on at 12:30 p.m. today. That is a song that's packed with a lot of punch . . . and persuasive power!

#temptingtostopwork #somebarsareopenatnoon

4) It is always 5:00 somewhere . . . and when a friend drops off a surprise package with a wine glass in it that says, "Surviving Quarantine One Sip at a Time," the temptation rises!

#after4oclock #butihaveanappointment

5) Restaurants and bars: One of our favorite places has reopened with outdoor seating and we stopped in for a drink, or two. It was hot. It was hot even under the canopy.

*#immelting #goodbeer #dinnertogo
#localrestaurant*

6) Masks: My favorite McDonald's drive-through supervisor even has a McDonald's mask.

#loveyourwork #wearitproud #drinkingofyou

7) Rock painting: This week's Be Social art kit from the park district was rock painting. My

son's masterpieces are set around in different places.

#likeaneasteregghunt #love #parkdistrict

8) Retirement: Facebook reminded me that it has been two years since I retired.

   #lifeisgood

9) Random thoughts: My friend posted a list of his random thoughts today. I didn't think that kind of thing could be so interesting!

   #whoknew

10) Picture upload: I posted more pictures today than usual, so I guess I am out of words. Good night!

   #rocks #drinks #pillows #excitinglife

Day 76

June 5, 2020

Signs of summer: Parallels to the Pandemic

1) Mosquitoes: They've obviously not learned social distancing or understand what wearing a mask means.

   #bullies

2) City Market: This is such a fabulous, local weekly event here in town, but this year will be so different.

   #inandoutmarket #nomusic #noseating
   #nomarketdining #vendors #stillneedsupport #go

3) Colorful fresh produce: I fixed Ratatouille tonight.

   #familynotafan #toomuchtomatostuff

4) Hanging flower baskets: They were 50% off at a nursery.

   #kindoflike #bogo

5) Bathing suits: A pair of gym shorts and a tank top make for a quick bathing suit.

   #whennooneisaround #hillbillysuit

6) Wet towels and suits: They are hanging here, there, and everywhere: patio chairs, wash line, kitchen chairs, kitchen bar stools, shower hooks, and over the bathtub.

#something #isalwaysdamp

7) Pool ambiance: Try as I might, I will never get my pool area to look and have that resort feel that everyone else's pool has.

#toomuchconcrete #toomuchspace
#mineislikeapublicpool #notaresort
#oldtimepotterystore #totherescue

8) Grill: It is what's for dinner.

#lambpatties #idontlikelamb
#turkeyburgerforme #ratatouilleleftovers

9) Air conditioner: I cannot hear you when I am turning on the garden hose over the sound of the air conditioner.

#staycool #putawaytheafghans

10) Long daylight: This is my time of year. I have two favorite seasons.

#summer #christmas

Have a good weekend.

Day 77

Summer Saturday: Parallels to the Pandemic

Most of my days start at the grocery store. I do a few orders and then I let the day go up for grabs.

1) Manicures: Who doesn't love a manicure and nice nails? Well, I do, but painted nails are such high maintenance, and my nails are pitiful. So, instead, I paint my left thumbnail because it is in so many pictures of the items I'm holding for a customer to consider as a substitute when items are out of stock. I was "air drying" my thumbnail on my 3-mile ride to the store this morning, only to be smudged when I couldn't get the customer's gate open when I delivered her groceries.

   #smdh #whydoibother

2) Belly buttons: I saw two ladies today whose clothing revealed the kind of belly button they have. One's shirt pulled in at the belly button spot, and the other was pushed out because she was about 8 months pregnant.

   #innies #outies #creepythatiwasnoticing

3) Dead-heading flowers: Tell me you can't resist dead-heading flowers on the way into Lowe's hardware store or other garden centers when you walk by them?

#meneither

4) Chick-Fil-A: Since we were going to Lowe's for the excitement of picking out a new kitchen sink, we decided to drive through Chick-Fil-A and eat in the car, in a parking lot, in the sun.

#nowthatdoesntsoundlikefun
#neitherdoesbuyingasink

5) Pampered Chef: My friend Elaine is having an on-line party so I browsed the catalog. Some people apparently buy gingerbread house molds. Are you kidding? Who in their right mind makes the crackers for gingerbread houses?

#buythekitfromthestore #swearandmutter
#underbreath #wholetime #theyarenotfun

6) Wine: My friend, Rhonda, dropped off a bottle of watermelon wine. I poured some in the glass that my friend Karen had given me. I think the whole bottle would fit in the glass!

#surivingquarentine #onesipatatime

7) Road trip: The plans are in the works to meet my daughter in Springfield, Illinois for lunch this week. Hurry up, Illinois! We would like

to eat inside a restaurant rather than under a tent or in a car.

#needphase4 #covid19

8) Feeding time: The baby birds in the nest were hungry, and the mama robin didn't care that I was watching.

#rockingrobin #tweettweet

9) Gigi's Playhouse: Shout out to everyone who participated in the Step to Accept fundraiser today. Well done!

#downsyndrome #amazingservices #localdollars

10) Ten at ten: I need to see what is on the 10:00 news.

#tvremote #challenged #needtime #togetitstarted

Buenos noches!

Day 78

Facebook reach: Parallels to the Pandemic

I am so grateful for the "reach" that Facebook provides. We can gain perspective from others that may otherwise not come up in a face to face conversation. We don't always know what's really going on in someone else's life, home, or heart. I read a post from a friend today that reminded me of how much we take for granted. I share more below, and I hope you will cheer for this remarkably simple, yet pivotal experience she celebrated today. (See #5).

Now, on to other ordinary things:

1) Hair: I'm a little gray, but not as much as I would think after these weeks without new color. There is a lot of "Marita" (my mom) in me, so I'm sure I'd be grayer if it continues to grow out much more. On the other hand, my husband thought it is getting long enough for a ponytail. A ponytail? I don't think I've ever worn a ponytail.

   #pigtails #braids #yes #notaponytail

2) Store coupons: I am all for using coupons, even clipped ones from the paper or the store's flyer, but hurry up already! If you are

going to use them, have the darn things ready to hand to the cashier BEFORE she is finished scanning all the groceries. Have your bank card in the other hand and finish the transaction and go!

#bigeyeroll #socialdistance
#otherwiseimighthavesaidsomething #notverynice

3) Sunday radio: A real old song came on this morning. "A Little Bitty Tear Let Me Down" (1961). Burl Ives. I would know that voice anywhere.

#hollyjollychristmas

4) White bread: Sometimes a meal just needs a piece of good, sliced white bread, even if it's not good for you. That would be beef stew.

#pepperidgefarm #farmhouseheartywhite

5) Autism: My friend, Elisa, posts about her son, Ethan. If you live with or love someone with autism, you will really understand and cheer this amazing moment. If you do not have much personal history with autism, this will give you a perspective on how such simple accomplishments are enormous wins. Today she wrote (and I shortened it a bit): "Ethan is very obsessed with menus. We have to have one or else he truly cannot function. Yesterday he saw oatmeal was on for today's breakfast. He wanted eggs. I said okay and told him he had to change the menu. He went to get it, and I heard him say "pen" in the kitchen as he retrieved it. He brought it to me, and I told him he had to do

it. He crossed off oatmeal. I told him to write EGGS. I directed him to write it in the box, but he could not do it due to his fine motor issues. Normally he writes hand over hand. BUT! He managed to write the word "egg" ALL BY HIMSELF, no hand over hand and stayed in the vicinity of the box! Then—last night before bed he said he wanted bacon too. I said yes, we could have bacon tomorrow. He came up to me real close and said, "bacon in the freezer." He was correct! He knew that before we went to bed I had to get the bacon out to thaw! Oh, my heart!"

#goethango

6) Dinner salad: The leftover spinach needed some add-ins to make a salad. So, I added peeled hard-boiled eggs on my grocery order today to speed things up.

#cheater

7) Sunday fun day: There's nothing like having your groceries delivered by one of your favorite shoppers and then having some "catch-up" time by the pool when she finished.

#lg #lifeisgood #shipt

8) Sneaky peeky: I ran into an acquaintance today and she mentioned reading my Top 10 lists every day. I told her I did not think we were friends on Facebook. She said she's

not on Facebook, but she reads through her daughter's page. I did laugh out loud.

#hilarious #whoelse #lurking

9) Small town love: My brother Doug just mentioned the local grocery store calls his father-in-law every week for his order and they deliver it. That is so cool!

#Bellevuelowa #notacomericalservice #takingcareoftheirown

10) Gratitude: Have you taken a moment to ponder all you have to be grateful for? Like my friend Elisa says, small things can be HUGE. Days are hard, challenges are many. I see you dear friend, you are amazing.

#somethingassimple #asamenuchange #breakthrough #celebrate

Day 79

June 8, 2020

Late update: Parallels to the Pandemic

Sometimes you must keep your word, even if it is working with metric measurements at 9 p.m. because you agreed to make the cake.

#smh

1) Shivers: Regardless, I will stay in the car until the song is over. Every. Single. Time. When you have witnessed a room full of cancer kids singing "It's a Great Day to Be Alive" you just stop in your tracks when you hear it.

   #shivers #smiles

2) McDonald's: I have been "holding it" for the past 2.5 months because I did not know you could go inside to place your order AND use the bathroom. A new day starts tomorrow!

   #publicbathrooms #scarse
   #enterrefreshmodeonthelid

3) Totally old school: Can you still buy a stenographer's pad?

   #whatsthat #uniquenotebook

4) Flew the coop: We're sure we saw the baby birds having their last supper yesterday. The nest was empty today.

   #enthralling

5) Pool time: My husband wondered if my tongue was sunburned because I fell asleep in the pool with my mouth open.

   #thatrelaxed.

6) Social Security: I had to make another dreaded call to their office today, but I put it off until extremely late in the afternoon ('til after my nap in the pool). Miracle. I was on and off the phone with a real person in less than 5 minutes.

   #superquickie

7) SMH: It is by far, my most favorite emoji. That is all.

   #shakingmyhead #idodumbthings #sometime

8) Recipe conversion: I am never sure how and why my son finds unusual recipes that always need conversion. It hurts my head. Between Google, a calculator, scrap paper, and looking up a similar recipe in a cookbook, I usually pull it off. But yi, yi, yi! Not at 9:00 at night.

   #justsayno

9) Double boiler: Recipes that call for a double boiler scare me off. Just like those that have yeast or hard/soft ball stage in them.

But without fail, my friend JoAnn always has some trick up her sleeve. A skillet and a saucepan work as a double boiler.

#genius #familyandconsumerscience #teacher

10) GTG: Time to unroll the sponge cake and finish up the cake.

#notimeforahashtag

Day 80

June 9, 2020

Shelter-in-Place: Parallels to the Pandemic

I put myself in a time-out today. There were things that needed to get finished that no one else will notice but me. But that is ok!

#feelingaccomplished

1) Afternoon office: I set up my afternoon office with a beverage and ambiance across from my son working at the kitchen table. Guess what song came on the radio?

   #yep #greatdaytobealive

2) Purging more files: I am not sure why we still had owner's manuals from dishwashers, microwaves, and DVD players we don't have anymore.

   #goodgrief #getridofit

3) Nostalgia: One of the files had a stack of chore lists I used to make for the kids. That was a blast from the past!

   #saturdaymornings #everybodydoyourshare

4) Masks: What in the world were disposable masks doing in a file in the file cabinet? Clueless!

   #mysonschemodays #maybe
   #butinafilecabinet #weird

5) Operation organization: I would probably drive you crazy if you saw how tidy the bottom two file cabinet drawers are now. Well, it may not drive my friend, Jennifer, crazy. She would be impressed that I have my colored paper and computer stationary all lined up in folders.

   #shegetsit

6) Hotel receipts: Our trip to Washington, D.C. was in 2009. We had a great rate at the Marriott/Metro Center thanks to connections. But really! I think it is safe to say there won't be any problems with the payment at this point and I can shred it.

   #leftmypillowthere #theysentitback

7) Library books: Took the plunge and went online to reserve a couple of books for curbside pick-up, but it did not quite turn out that way. Instead, I clicked on "adult book requests" and through the survey they will select books for you.

   #soundsalittleperverted #librarybooksurprise

8) CARES Act: After going through some financial things today, I realized we are receiving

an exemption/deferment on the kids' student loans.

#payattention #thanks #butnothanks #covid19

9) Give Kids the World (GKTW): This resort is in Kissimee, Florida, and is a referral-based location for families who have a child with chronic/life threatening/debilitating conditions. Sheri, another cancer mom friend of mine, shared an article that it is closed until further notice to protect the vulnerable children they serve. Like so many other things that have been robbed by COVID-19. Some of these kids will not be living when GKTW can reopen. My heart breaks. It is an amazing partner organization with agencies like the Make-A-Wish foundation.

#wewerethere #nineteenninetyeight
#makeawishtrip

10) Road trip: Matt and I are going on a road trip tomorrow. My husband has assured me "all systems are go" with his DVD/blue ray player.

#chargedbattery #correctadaptors #fingerscrossed

Shelter-in-place is not such a bad thing. I should do it more often. I got so much accomplished today.

Day 81

Road trip: Parallels to the Pandemic

Matt and I took a road trip to Springfield, Illinois, today to have lunch with my daughter and a friend of hers. The Top 10 things that set this day apart from others:

1) Big day: It called for earrings, a necklace, pretty sandals, AND lipstick.

   #boyohboy #escapefromthenorm

2) "Do you have your mask?" – This was the last thing I said to Matt before we got in the car. Under normal conditions, I would have said something like "Do you have the DVD adapter?"

   #crazytalk #hereadabookinstead

3) Miles: The trek between our home and Bloomington, Illinois is so boring! Note to self: bring peppermints along next time.

   #alert #conferencecandybowls #tokeepyouawake

4) Caffeine: I abstained from caffeine this morning so I could have a soda with lunch.

   #notacoffeedrinker #singwithradioinstead

5) Lincoln Exit 126: This is my favorite stop on the way, but unfortunately, you are almost to Springfield when it comes up. The Russell Stover candy store has lots of chocolate and the bargains are crazy fun. I bought chocolate peanut butter valentines to pass out to my co-workers and a box of Bloopers for a special group of people.

   #chocolate #neveroutofstyle

6) Finley's: We met Carrie and her friend for lunch and were seated indoors. That was unique as there are very few restaurants in Rockford that can have indoor dining yet.

   #horseshoeonthemenu #wheninspringfield.

7) USMLE Step 1: Shout out to Tyler, my daughter's boyfriend, who is taking the U.S. Medical Licensing exam tomorrow. It is the first test towards becoming a physician.

   #gotylergo #rotationsaftertest

8) Walmart: Matt still had a gift card from Christmas. He told Carrie that he was going to buy bagels and clothes. And he did just that. The fitting rooms were closed, so he improvised and used the men's restroom. I did not realize that was what he was doing until I heard an employee mention this to him.

   #oops #securityguardundercover
   #advisedbyotheremployee #nbd

9) Masks: Holey C'moley! There were so many people who were not wearing masks in the Springfield Walmart.

#shocked #old #young #middleaged
#families #waymorecasual

10) More miles: The dashboard panel tells you when you need to take a rest. And the orange light signals that you need gas. Note to self: Take the Toyota next time.

#husbandscar #gastank #toosmall

There are more trips to Springfield in our future. Carrie is moving there when her job starts in late summer.

Day 82

June 11, 2020

Thoughts from a pretty uneventful day: Parallels to the Pandemic

1) Receipts: If your store receipt is not at the top in the garbage can, or slightly lower, Old Time Pottery probably doesn't want the receipt back anyway.

   #instorecredit #spentmorethanreturn

2) Neighborhood walkers: I enjoy my front room's great view of the people who walk in the neighborhood. I always hope my neighbors, Beth and Armour, don't stop and ask me to go with them.

   #theywalktoofast #outofbreath

3) Library curbside pick-up: It all went great with my library request. I felt like I was receiving a sterilized instrument from the operating room. The book was in a brown paper bag, stapled and tagged with my name, the book title, and return date, and pushed out to me on a metal cart by a masked "technician."

   #evviedrakestartsover #adultbookrequest

4) Era ends: My daughter packed the last of her belongings in her car, said goodbye to her dear roommate, and left Columbia, Missouri. This sort of makes me sad. Life as she knows it is about to change, but in a big, good way.

#mizzou #undergradalum #mastersalum #adulting

5) COVID-19 patients: I only know a few people who have tested positive for the coronavirus, but the personal stories I have heard are devastating.

#thisisreal #butschoolsmustopen

6) Turkey burgers vs hamburgers: Honestly, I can't really tell the difference when they're cooked on the grill. But why is a hamburger called a hamburger when it's not made out of ham?

#deepthoughts #prettybored #tonight

7) The stuff I have saved: I had the coolest paint jars, brushes, and paint dishes from when the kids were little and painted on easels. I saved the brushes and the dishes and totally got my kicks out of using them today.

#twentyyearslater #butthosebeaniebabies

8) Day 82: From when I started counting the days when the governor ordered the Shelter-in-Place directive, I am on Day # 82. It was the first business day of such. As I approach #100, I am sitting on the fence. 100 seems

like a good place to stop and a new place to start something else.

#getserious #aboutwriting #abookwithchapters

9) Day 101: Since I have established a regular practice of writing, even if it is only a crazy list of Top 10 things on an ordinary day, writing something more substantial might be a good thing to continue. But first the state must end "work from home" so my husband can return to his office. I don't think I can write anything serious with his daily newspaper crowding me at this desk.

#otherdeskclutter #excuses #excuses #excuses

10) Babble: Ok, I am finished babbling. I made it to 10. Atta girl! Atta boy! Pat yourself on the back if you read all the way through today.

#highfive #applause

Day 83

Fri-yay: Parallels to the Pandemic

Fri-yay: I have never used that word, but it's kind of fun to say. Fridays in the summer generally meant the start of lots of fun things for the weekend. But this summer is way different. Kind of boo-yay instead!

1) Inflation: A glass of lemonade at a kid's neighborhood stand was a dollar. I really, really wanted to support it. I had 75 cents in change and nothing smaller than a five-dollar bill. I just could not throw my $5 in.

   #donatedmychange #tightwad

2) Tinnitus:

   #selfdiagnosed

3) City Market: Unfortunately, this has been scaled down so much this summer. I felt compelled to buy something, so I got a roll-on insect repellent that I did not really need. The temperature dropped 10 degrees in an hour, so instead of shivering we went home.

   #bust

4) Wearing earrings: Since I have lost earrings a few times from taking a mask on and off, I haven't worn them in a while. I thought I would be all classy tonight to go to the city market and put on a pair of "dangly" earrings. Well, that lasted about 25 minutes.

#ouch #covid19problems

5) Spray paint: They even make it in clear matte or glossy spray. Who knew? Everything that's yard art here is getting a fresh coat or two.

#ilovespraypaint #bff

6) Taco Betty's: When we walked past their outdoor dining area tonight, the server called out to us. She remembered us from trivia nights last summer.

#locals #cheers

7) Hand sanitizer: I guess the panic is over and the supply is meeting the demand. There were five choices today for an order.

#thingsthatgetyouexcited #shiptshopper

8) Pool time: The timing of the sun and the pool was impeccable today. So glad to have friends over this afternoon.

#friends #oldhood #socialdistance

9) Head in hand: When you sit at the computer with head in hand and stare out the window

trying to think of #9 and #10, it is time to stop.

#shortlist #tonight

10) Food at City Market: My son had the pulled pork nachos, my husband had chicken pad Thai and I had the Korean barbeque chicken sandwich. When all else fails to fill the list of Top 10, resort to "what's for dinner?"

#or #weathertalk

So, there is Fri-yay wrapped up at 9:10 pm. I am going to bed to read my library book. I wonder if I will get a gold star on a chart somewhere for a summer reading program when I finish the book.

#summerfun #askids

Day 84

June 13, 2020

Summer days: Parallels to the Pandemic

I love the long days of summer, but gosh, it sure seems like a long time ago since it was morning! Today's fun:

1) Watermelon: My favorite way to cut it is in spears. Now if I could just pick out a melon with great flavor.

   #diy #cutspears

2) Goodwill: I usually drop off clothing donations at one of three places. Honestly, Goodwill is the easiest, most efficient, and convenient to home. I didn't even have to get out of my car.

   #otherplaces #goodtoo

3) Spray paint: Here I go again, carrying on about spray paint. But if there is any way to get quick satisfaction for completing a project, break out the spray paint!

   #sunart #butterflyart

4) Highway department: Apparently, they thought painting was fun, too. They have finally repainted the lane stripes and curb

lines on a major road in town. Now maybe I can see where in the world I am at night by the Walgreens near our home. And when it rains at night . . . oh good Lord, help me!

#spatialorientation #problems #stayinyourlane

5) McDonald's: Matt and I went inside today to order our drinks since the drive-through line was so long. The red and yellow hearts in their window to make the letter "M" logo was original.

#imlovingit

6) Quick, look! All the flowers in the front bed were in bloom at the same time this morning. Would you bet that it will only last for a few days?

#nojunebugs

7) Masks: I am even more impressed with seeing so many people wearing masks at the grocery store, especially since it seemed less prevalent in Springfield this week.

#Meijergrocerystore
#evenifyoudontagree #coverup

8) Church: Our church can accommodate up to 200 people with the re-opening for Mass. The procedures are written up in the bulletin, including: "Unfortunately, we will be unable to congregate or visit in the narthex after Mass, but we can wave at each other."

#hineighbor #socialdistancing

9) Meal prep: I washed dishes twice today and ran the dishwasher once. I don't think I need to do that so soon again!

   #hireacook #buymoredishsoap

10) Fill in the blank: No #10 tonight. Your turn:

Day 85

June 14, 2020

Sunday: A day of rest—Parallels to the Pandemic

I am taking the day off. See you tomorrow.

Day 86

Untitled: Parallels to the Pandemic

This was a day to head out of Dodge!

1) Service Master, we have a problem: Someone at our place forgot to turn the hose off yesterday while watering a bush and it ran for an exceedingly long time. It leaked into the basement and we had a soggy mess. Thank you to our friend, David, for hooking us up so quickly with Service Master!

   #noitwasntme #carpetedbasement #nolonger

2) Friends: I met with some friends for a long-overdue visit while my husband dealt with the water mess at home.

   #leaveyourproblemsathome #retiredteacherfriends

3) Quarantine: My guys pretty much are home all the time. I try to think of places where I can go with my son, even if it is to Beloit, Wisconsin, a mere 30 minutes away.

   #beerrun #gpstobeloit #spottedcowbeer

4) Masks in Beloit: Masks are required at the regional grocery story, Woodman's, as expected, but not in our car.

#rules #confusing #formyson

5) Break-out: Since we broke out of the house today, we stopped at The Rock Bar and Grill in Beloit. It has a great river view, good beer, and great appetizers. The pickle out of my son's "Frickle" sandwich slid out and onto the ground.

#itsalwayssomething #forgoshsakes

6) Summer void: This would have been our twelfth season of Buddy Baseball. I started this program with the park district in 2009. I have been doing little with it these past few years but am starting to feel the void of going out to the ballpark to see all the kids and their buddies having fun.

#parentstoo #covid19 #makesmesad

7) Meal plan: My son is at it again. This week we are going to make an onion ring loaf. I guess we need to have something interesting and new to do while there isn't much else to do.

#yes #onionringloaf #thereissuchathing #apparently

8) Store exchanges: It seems some stores (Walmart) aren't taking returns yet, at least on clothing, due to the pandemic precautions. Not everything that Matt tried on in

the bathroom at the Springfield Walmart last week was a good fit.

#tshirt #illinoislogo #toosmall #whowantsit

9) Shelter-in-Place: I am still cleaning out files. The time at home has been good for this project. There is no need to keep stuff that had our former address on it.

#seventeen #yearsago #myson #mastershredder

10) Social Security fear: I won't part with Matt's receipts, documents, etc. until they're past seven years old. Surely, Social Security will want something if I don't have them, so I am keeping it all.

#murphyslaw #keepeverything #sherionsteroids

Day 87

Randomness: Parallels to the Pandemic

1) I saw a meme that says "Who wants to have a New Year's Eve party on June 30th and pretend the first half of the year was just a bad dream? I'll bring margaritas!" I'm in!

   #iwillbringbeer

2) Child's play: Forget fidget spinners. We had clackers back in the day!

   #louder #faster

3) McDonald's: Chocolate chip cookies are back!

   #160calories #dietcoke #itsawash #drinkingofyou

4) Trauma-sensitive flower care: The "wintered" geraniums are finally recovering from being inside to outside.

   #resilience

5) Curbside library service: Sweet Charity DVD (1969).

   #mysonsrequest #shirleymaclaine

#sammydavisjunior

6) Masks: Happy hour with my friend, Sandy.

#aeroalehouse #patio #mymaskhadcowsonit

7) Lion's Club Rose Day: My son will be happy to take your order.

#delivery #twentydollar #donation

8) Haircut: Some of the best conversations are with your hairdresser. Right?

#yes

9) Phone apps: My phone screens drive my daughter nuts.

#toomanyapps #usefolders

10) Countdown: Hitting 100 days of Shelter-in-Place/Parallels to the Pandemic daily list is 13 days away. Technically, that will be June 29. Perhaps I will push it 'til June 30, so the final day of June is not left in quarantine by itself. Then I will go to that New Year's Eve party.

#seenumber1

Day 88

June 17, 2020

FWIW: Parallels to the Pandemic

Psst: Mom . . . FWIW means "for what it's worth." Here is a peek at what went on today.

1) Our park district delivers fun. Always! They dropped off the next craft kit for their virtual programming.

    #mosaictile

2) Invite friends for dinner, make a list, and know that cleaning the bathrooms never gets scratched off the list.

    #ohwell #nojudgementfriends #triviateam

3) Since we had company for dinner, it feels like it is the weekend.

    #asmysonsays #humpday

4) We would stand the best chance of getting a prize in our neighborhood for having the most service workers at our place in one week.

    #rotorooter #awaygoestroubledownthedrain #youaresingingit #yes

5) The flowers were so pretty I had to bring them in. Just like my mom always did.

   #himom

6) Masks: Yep, still always something about the masks. Most people have some functional mask, but there is always that one person. An adult man in the store today had his t-shirt pulled up over his nose and mouth. Like kids do when someone passes gas.

   #gobacktothirdgrade

7) Hand sanitizer: The stores are stocked again and sanitizer is not going off the shelves very quickly. Now Clorox wipes, that is still another story.

   #shopper

8) I ordered groceries because I needed a kid's beach bucket and shovel to make a Bucket 'O Ooze for a dessert tomorrow. My shopper had to sub a gallon of ice cream for it because that was the closest thing to a bucket that the store had. Then I had to find containers big enough to store the ice cream, so I could use the empty bucket.

   #kidscoming #swim #fun

9) A friend stopped in to purchase Lion's Club roses. That was a fun surprise!

   #twodozen #buyforyourself #buyforsomeoneelse

10) Question (seriously): Do you think the plexi-glass shields will remain in place at cashier

stations when we are finished with "this stuff"?

#hopenot #covid19

Day 89

June 18, 2020

Friends and family day: Parallels to the Pandemic
It is summer. Work a little, play a lot.

1) My daughter is home! Yay! She is in between now and what is to come.

   #springfieldillinois #latesummer #healthsystems

2) Carrie's interim work: Shipt! She has shopped in Columbia, MO, Springfield IL, and now Rockford for a few months.

   #gocarriego #portablework #likemotherlikedaughter

3) Grab some fun! My friend Kara came with her kids and her dear sister and my sweet friend, Laren, to swim today. It was so fun having kids in the pool again.

   #splishsplash

4) Bucket 'O Ooze: I found a plastic bucket and shovel, instead of using the ice cream bucket, to make our treat today. So easy, so good.

   #pudding #coolwhip #vanillawafers #ez

5) Game time at the pool: UNO and Guess Who with Laren and Matt helps keep their fair skin out of the sun.

   #redheads #UNOneverends #drawfour

6) More fun with friends! My friend, Cara, came over with her friend, Janie, for some water therapy.

   #havenoodle #willfloat

7) The City Market has been approved to add some tables and chairs to the event . . . and a local beer distributor.

   #socialdistance #beer #itreallyissummer

8) Too much play time today, no #8)

   #slacker

9) Work harder tomorrow to make a longer list.

   #hihohiho

10) Do you have any day trips or vacations planned this summer?

   #moststatesstillclosed

Day 90

June 19, 2020

The 90's—Parallels to the Pandemic

Today starts the last "ten" of the Shelter-in-Place and the Parallels to the Pandemic. Here we go . . .

1) Forgiveness: Petunias will forgive you if you water them. If you water them a lot.

   #callme #girlwiththewateringcan #famouspainting #Renoir

2) Proof: My friend, Jay, said if there were not pictures it did not happen. Well, it happened today. I was in the pool.

   #perfectpoolday

3) McDonald's: Is it faster to wait in the drive-through line or go in the lobby to order?

   Action #1: notice which car you would be behind if you were going through the drive line (red car).

   Action #2: go in and use the bathroom.

   Action #3: order a Diet Coke at the counter.

   Action #4: pay with a McDonald's gift card (cashless transaction). Experience a break in the action/progress: Wait and wait and wait for someone to fill a cup with Diet Coke. Roll my eyes.

Action #5: ask if someone can get the cup of pop.

Action #6: learn that there is only one pop machine and it is filled as orders are received. If a drive-through order had a Diet Coke they could have given me that one. Eye roll again.

Action #7: receive pop and exit.

Action #8: notice where the red car is in the drive-through line. It is next in line to pay.

Results/Conclusion: It is just as fast to stay in a longer drive-through line than go in to order if you don't have to go to the bathroom.

#onepopmachine #noselfserve #covid19

4) Long red lights: Sitting at a long red light is the cause of exceeding individual serving sizes.

#twizzlerbites #thirteenpiecesisservingsize #probabyhad20pieces

5) Outdoor dining: When the website says there's no outdoor dining, but you don't quite believe them because they have a large picnic area, you pack a tablecloth just in case.

#bbq #outdoors #brisketsandwiches

6) Informal education: There's nothing like a young medical student gaining knowledge of middle-aged women problems in one easy afternoon while sitting around the pool.

#priceless #youguesswhoisthemedstudent

7) Citronella candles: Question: How many citronella candles do you need for the summer? Answer: Four. Two from the pool storage shed, one from the pool bathroom shelves and a new one from Bed, Bath and Beyond because you're sure one of the wicks in the other candles won't work this year.

    #iwasright #onewontlight

8) Crazy 8: There's something about #8 on this Top Ten List. I go blank. About as random as I can get, here are 8 things that clutter the computer desk from which I am working: doctor referral promotion cards, a screw, a water glass, a picture from junior high of a friend and me, a useless keyboard vacuum, a list of my son's passwords, dental floss, and dust.

    #eyespy #withmylittleeye

9) Travel plans: My daughter and I are discussing where to reschedule the trip we were going to take on her spring break.

    #scratchNYC #SanAntonio #contender

10) 10:00 at #10 Time to call it a day.

    #goodnight

Day 91

June 20, 2021

Time: Parallels to the Pandemic

When you spend too much time thinking of a title for today's list, it is not important. Move along.

1) Time management: Today was a little lop-sided with work and play. There are still dinner dishes to finish before the night is over since we played all day.

   #potsandpans #mattsrecipe

2) Podcasts: Well, I don't really listen to podcasts, but I figured I could grab your attention by phrasing this one with a cool word. The "podcasts" I listen to when driving are Gerry Brooks' take on all things relative to people who work in schools.

   #veryfunny #principal #3minutesoflaughs

3) Gerry Brooks: The funniest ones I listened to today were "How to Open Schools in the Fall" and "Interview Season for Educators."

   #spoton

4) Errand: I ran an errand for a friend today and absolutely loved my drive down the

gravel lane. It was like a little bit of country in the city.

#likegirlscoutcamp

5) Recipe night: Matt's discovered recipe for onion ring loaf finally worked into the dinner plan tonight. Yeah, better idea, just make the onion rings and skip the "loaf." Even better, order onion rings from the Schwann's man again.

#dinnerdishes #inthesink #seenumberone

6) Twins: The onion ring loaf called for three eggs to make the batter. One egg had two yolks. That was weird. I wonder what the science/biology is behind that irregular phenomenon.

#identical #notfraternal

7) Cheetos: There was a snack box for delivery people on the porch at one of my deliveries this morning. This was so common around the holidays, but not lately. I picked Cheetos because they are truly a secret indulgence.

#afterdietcoke #butthatsnotasecret #orangefingers

8) McDonald's: Not today! Instead, I went out of my way to go to a Steak and Shake so I could use up the balance on a gift card that was my husband's at Christmas. It sat on the counter for just long enough. SMH. They gave me the wrong kind of pop.

#figures #dontchangeyourroutine

9) Sushi: I noticed a new restaurant in town as I sat in line at the Steak and Shake. I have no idea if it is open or not. It's an all you can eat sushi joint.

   #dontlikesushi #fka #rubytuesdays

10) Father's Day tomorrow: We are going over the state line for lunch.

   #beloitwisconsin #lucysbar7 #caneatindoors

Good night.

Day 92

Father's Day: Parallels to the Pandemic

There are so many great dads out there—past, present, and future! I know there are many people who have had very difficult relationships with their dad, but I hope there has been someone else in their life who has been a pillar of strength, love and understanding. And hats off to all the moms who are the dad AND the mom in their family. I am sending them a huge COVID-19 elbow hug with many warm thoughts.

1) My dad: He raised five kids with my mom, loved the Cubs, coached Little League, walked all three of us girls down the aisle, loved all his kids and their spouses, was employed as a school bus driver and custodian for their local school district for many years, cried easily, and loved my mom for over 55 years.

    #geneoberbroeckling #myhero

2) My husband: He is raising/raised three kids with me, stood strong with resilience during the challenge and heartbreak of our lifetime, served in the US Navy, likes a good history documentary, doesn't need fancy cars or

million-dollar houses, just a good beer or bourbon once in a while.

#gregwhite #myhero

3) Celebration: We had lunch at Lucy's Bar 7 in Beloit, WI to celebrate Father's Day. In my husband's words: It was so nice to be somewhere "normal." That is code for eating inside a restaurant, not wearing masks, and going about as business as usual.

#happyfathersday #easytoplease

4) Handwriting: I have often wondered how old one would be when their handwriting starts to look like an old lady's. I guess it is 61. My daughter said she could barely read my list of beers for my beer flight at lunch today.

#ohgoodgrief #betterthanagingspots #servercouldreadit

5) Worship: Church is "open" with restrictions and precautions. My husband reserved a space for us, as I have admitted, church on TV in our living room did not work for me. Worship inside the church is much better. But it is so weird having the priest wear a mask while saying Mass.

#doctors #lookbetterinmasks

6) Be Not Afraid: That song from church gets me every time. It's a trigger from one day, a long time ago, when I was able to get away to go to church when Matt was very sick. "Be not afraid, I go before you always" . . .

a friend reached out to me after Mass with a hug and some comforting words. I have not seen her in a long time, but "showing up" in that moment was just what I needed. My prayer for my friends who are grieving or struggling tonight is "Be not afraid, I go before you always . . . I will give you rest".

#itshard #veryhard

7) Ok, let's lighten up: #6 was a little more than I usually offer, but it is Sunday and all.

#amen

8) Dinner menu: Nothing unique this week.

#justsayno #makeeasystuff #orderout

9) Masks: Nothing to report but a question to ask: Where do you get your masks? What kind are they?

#covid19

10) Bugs Bunny: Th–th–that's all, folks!

Day 93

June 22, 2020

We keep going: Parallels to the Pandemic

Rarely has there been anything on our calendar for the past three months. Things are starting up again with the usual, ordinary things: dentist appointments, day trips, etc. We are looking forward to Phase 4 of the recovery plan.

1) Volunteer: The calendar in my phone reminds me that I have a volunteer commitment at Swedish American Hospital on Tuesdays. Other than that reminder, it doesn't even dawn on me that I would usually have that time scheduled.

   #closedtovolunteers

2) Serger: My mom used to do tons of sewing, quilting, etc. When she moved to her apartment here in Illinois, she gave me her Serger sewing machine. The most use it has had here is using the box it's in as a stand for the paper shredding pile. My daughter is going to take it back to my mom tomorrow so she can do some projects.

   #gomomgo

3) Costco: I am a terrible member. I have been there once since I took out a membership in March. But I now have 1000 dinner napkins and enough toilet paper to last till kingdom comes.

   #crazysizes #onesize #doesnotfitall

4) Love is: when your husband washes your cloth mask and uses Spray and Wash to pre-treat all the make-up on the inside of it.

   #thelittlethings #wearomantic

5) Masks: Now Hanes is in on the action and they have manufactured masks. That would be like wearing your underwear on your face.

   #tightywhities

6) Listerine: My husband said that Listerine is advertising for "mask-breath."

   #omg #covid19

7) TikTok: One of my summer goals is to make a TikTok video. I am not sure why, but it seems like it's what the cool cats are doing.

   #iwanttobecooltoo #mykids #rollingtheireyes

8) Raise your hand: Or throw up a "like" if you have been reading along but haven't commented or replied with an emoji over these past 93 days. It's been fun to hear/see who has been reading. Social media is good for connecting, and it's been fun to share/chat with you during this pandemic.

   #anylurkers #outthere #thankyou #faithfulreaders

#thishasbeenfun #eightmoredays

9) Too long: #8 was too many lines so #9 is short.

#9isfine

10) Short: #10 is shorter than #9

#goodnight

See you tomorrow.

Day 94

Boring: Parallels to the Pandemic

Day 94 will not go down in history. It would be crazy to tell you how much time I spent on the computer getting nothing accomplished to reschedule a trip. So, let's talk about some other things.

1) Can't read lips: A man in a red van going down State Street today blasted his horn at me, but I couldn't make out what he was saying. I think it was something like, "Put the phone DOWN!"

   #yessir #shameonme

2) Christmas all year: It is fine with me if you keep cool Christmas decorations up all year . . . on a sheltered porch.

   #christmasinsummer #whoisyoursanta

3) Not worth it: Bagels and cream cheese are not my choice for breakfast or lunch, but Matt likes them. A lox bagel will work though for me, but don't sub whipped cream cheese spread for the real cream cheese. Whipped is easier to spread, but not worth it.

   #nasty #bestusedby #may21st #throwitout

4) Lunch: I did something today that my dad always did when he sold Watkins. I took my lunch (lox bagel) to a deserted park and sat on a bench and read a few pages in my book. I was killing time until my dentist appointment but ended up in the car since it was cool.

   #nooner

5) Pumping: The highlight of my day was sitting in my car at the park with my lunch and book, watching a grandma coach her granddaughter on how to "pump" her swing to go higher as she pushed her.

   #simplelife #lazydaysofsummer
   #guessyouhadtobethere

6) Desperate: As I reach and stretch for something to add to this list, I thought I would show you a picture of a stick-on wiggly eye that was stuck to my foot this morning . . . .somewhere from getting out of bed and out of the shower. Those silly craft project materials hide out all over the house. It fell off my foot sometime mid-morning. It probably thought my day was too boring to hang around. (EDITED: I took down the photo, too weird).

   #ewww #wigglyeyecrafts #afewweeksago

7) Shout out: A few friends jumped in last night that I didn't know were following along on

my daily posts. Thank you for that! Who else has been quiet out there?

#dontbeshy #gladyouarehere

8) More lunch news: My daughter went in to see my mom today and they went out for lunch. Mom's apartment building has been on lockdown so it was good that she could get out for a while.

    #panera

9) Sourdough hobby: Carrie is feeding a jar of stuff to make sourdough bread.

    #interesting #lookslike #papermache

10) Straying away from intended purpose: There's not much on this list today that resembles shelter-in-place or pandemic related issues. Well, maybe the fact that I was on the wrong day for when my dentist is opening again, but that was my error.

    #openingsoon #backtonormal #sortof

It's not even 10 pm and I'm already finished. How about that??!!

Day 95

June 24, 2020

Persons of interest: Parallels to the Pandemic

Some people in a day's time make me smile, on the inside and the outside. Here is today:

1) Robert M.—The "people counter" at Meijer. This is probably his first job and he looked so spiffy in his new Sperry-like shoes, fresh Dockers, and navy-blue polo shirt. If I knew his mom, I would tell her I was as proud of him as she probably is. And he is getting a new puppy . . . just so you know.

   #professionalresume #startsnow

2) McDonald's drive-through cashier—I didn't get this young guy's name because I was too flustered. I was digging for near-exact change and he insisted on paying for my order. There wasn't even anyone behind me in line so there wasn't any hurry. $2.61. A cheeseburger and a Diet Coke. That was probably a little chunk for him to throw in.

   #coinshortage #unitedstates #covid19

3) Robyn C.—Administrative coordinator for Matt's home-based funding waiver. She immediately looked into a matter and resolved a small issue for us in lightning speed.

#appreciateher

4) The guy in the overalls—No name on this guy and he didn't really make me smile in such a nice way, but I did snicker. As I passed him with my cart (going the wrong way) in the main grocery aisle, I heard him mutter under his breath, "Follow the damn arrows." Then there was more muttering, and I could tell his day wasn't off to such a great start.

#cutmesomeslack #plentyofroom

5) Tyler—My daughter's boyfriend received great scores today on his exam.

#bringiton #nextlevel

6) Kelly S.—My liaison for tech support: She is working the angles to help me get a device cleaned up for re-gifting.

#sheknowspeople

7) Shannon S.—Park District: Since Buddy Baseball is cancelled this season, she's posting pictures each week of previous years.

#inauguralseason #sofun #memorylane
#parkdistrict #rocks

8) Cara F.—My friend invited me to join her for Wine Night at another friend's house.

#hadtopass #nicetobeasked

9) Public Library workers—They expedited our request and "bundled" our materials, so I didn't have to go back tomorrow for the other one.

#read20minutes #orwatchaDVD #guesswhogotwhat

10) Persons of interest—Who are yours?

#circleofinfluence

Day 96

Signs: Parallels to the Pandemic
I'm not psychic, but signs are fun, literally and figuratively.

1) Notify in case of emergency: I put my daughter's name as next of kin on some of Matt's paperwork today instead of my sister's name.
    #figurativesign #timeshavechanged

2) Garage sale: There were several signs posted out and about today which have been generally absent this spring and summer.
    *#thingsareresuming #phasefour
    #tomorrow #covid19*

3) Rummage sale: The annual rummage sale at the church down on the corner is outdoors this year. That is highly unusual (and hot wearing a mask in 82° sun) and is a sign that we are still in the throes of coronavirus prevention.
    *#boughtspraypaint #wastedfiftycents
    #nonozzleincan*

4) Carpentry work: We're in the second phase of the new countertop experience. Eric, a

friend of ours, brought the Sawzall and went to work. This is a sign that if you know a guy with tools and skills, stuff happens.

#whoopwhoop

5) Flowers: I see so many amazing flower gardens throughout the day, but one really struck me today. I felt it was a sign to slow down, find peace, and take in all that is beautiful. It reminded me of my old Ideals magazines from once upon a time.

#idealsmagazine #manystacksofthem

6) Bee Crossing sign: Yes, I saw a sign today that said Bee Crossing. There's a right of way for all of God's creatures. I hope the bees stay in their own lane all summer.

#stockbenadryl #stockraid

7) Second wind: It is definitely a sign that you should change your plans when you reach in the refrigerator for a soft drink, but the Coors Light can says "Chill."

#noshame #fiveoclocksomewhere

8) Take-out containers: Red Lobster was "what's for dinner" tonight and it was apparent the plastic containers weren't going to be useful as freezer containers for future to-go meals. It is a sign I may need more Ziploc containers.

#airventsinlids #mysisters
#sayrecycletakeoutdishes #wellallright

9) Late night news: As a kid, when the 10:00 news came on, the announcer always said: "Parents, where are your children?" That was a sign that parents best account for their kids and get them to bed. It's that time right now.

#goodnight #notakidanymore #bedtimeanyway

10) Over and out: That's your sign. This list is finished, and the day is done.

#sweetdreams #gutenacht

Day 97

June 26, 2020

This one is different: Parallels to the Pandemic

I did not know.

I did not know that today:

I would be sitting in a reclining theater chair trying to figure out the switches to make it work.

I would be watching a movie about something that struck so close to home and my heart.

I would have tears rolling down my cheeks that went all the way down my neck.

I would be watching such a solid love story that ended so quickly.

I would secretly identify with the dad's feelings of disappointment and dashed dreams, but knowing our lives are full because of them.

I would wonder if this was a sign that it is time to write our story.

So, today's post is different. There might be 10 things in that list, I haven't counted. But I feel like I am cheating because it is nothing about the pandemic. I could add one thing to make it legit. We did wear masks. (There is always something about the masks!)

#datewithmyson #lindotheater
#freeportillinois #istillbelieve #jeremycamp
#story #herlastjournalentry #writethestory
#benotafraid #itsmysign

Day 98

June 27, 2020

Saturday WOWS: Parallels to the Pandemic

1) Soft Scrub cleanser: It should come with a large spot on the label that says: "Caution— This is concentrated. Less is more." I could have taken a bubble bath in my kitchen sink.

   #easygirl #tinysquirt #allyouneed

2) Morning Glories:

   #ilovepurple

3) Anything cold in a cooler by the pool.

   #summershandy #spottedcow #kolsch #diettcoke #water #raspberrytea

4) Friends bringing leftover Portillo's chocolate cake.

   #omg #sotasty

5) Fresh flowers from a friend's garden.

   #beebalm

6) Fourth of July napkins: Fifty cents at the church garage sale.

#letfreedomring

7) My son's menu planning from the internet: souffle, veggie soup, pot roast.

#soundslike #easyweek

8) Pool pictures: Seeing our pool show up on a friend's timeline.

#lifeisgood

9) Turkey pesto burgers on the grill: This is our summer "go-to" made with fresh ground turkey, fresh spinach, pesto, topped with a grilled pineapple ring and a slice of provolone cheese served on a toasted bun.

#delicious

10) Gummies: A friend asked if I have ever tried gummies. Gummy bears? Duh. No, not those kinds of gummies.

#iamnaive #lol #legalinillinois

Day 99

June 28, 2020

99/104: Parallels to the Pandemic

99/104 is not a backwards blood pressure reading. It's how many days you've/we've/I have been counting since the pandemic pretty much shut things down and changed the way we do life. I started from the first business day, so I am on Day #99. Matt counts from the day the governor issued the Shelter-in-Place order on Friday, March 13, so he's on #104. It could technically be 104 days. Either way, my 100 days are coming to an end. In the meantime, this will be brief tonight.

1) Vacuuming and electronic picture files: A little housekeeping late at night uncovers some great finds! While I was vacuuming, I came across a basket with reading lights in it and a handwritten letter from my dad. Then I found a cool picture in my electronic picture files from when the kids were little.

   #dearolddadletter #relayforlife1999picture

2) There's really nothing else that I can think of that would be worthy of this list.

   #eleventhirtyatnight #tootired #seeyoutomorrow

Day 100

DAY #100: Shelter-in-Place and Parallels to the Pandemic

Well, here we are. Day 100. Reaching a goal that was never intended to be a goal. So weird how that happened. It has been great bringing you along for the ride and relating to the inconveniences the coronavirus has caused. Gratefully, our families have not been directly affected or impacted by it. We need to keep washing our hands, wearing masks, and practicing social distance. It matters.

I have one more day to write, because if a calendar date had a heart and a brain, it might feel left out since all the other days in June were included in the set. Here's a few things to mention from today.

1) The parking lot: A woman approached me in the parking lot this morning at Target and asked for money for food. I don't usually oblige, but in light of all that has gone on (even though one really has nothing to do with the other unless COVID-19 has caused her some financial hardships), my conscience bothered me, so I did. I only had one bill in my wallet, a ten-dollar bill. Oh, that was tough to give up, but I so desperately wanted her to go to Aldi to get some food as she said

she would. As I loaded my car, I watched her talking to another person. I was in a bit of a hurry, but I told her that Aldi was already open. She said she was going there. I waited and watched her walk into the store but did not wait to see if she walked right back out. I had made the decision to give her money; it was her decision to do the right thing. If I was a sucker, so be it. If I had given it more than a second's thought, I could have taken the money to Aldi myself and given it to the cashier for the woman's groceries.

#nexttimepayforthegroceries #mydeliverygratuity #twicewhatigaveaway #karma

2) McDonald's: The cashier stations inside now have plexiglass dividing each register. So bizarre. As I left with my Diet Coke, the song on their soundtrack was "Killing Me Softly" (Fugees/Roberta Flack). I had to linger for just a minute.

#lovethatsong #highschoolboyfriend #feelingbubbly

3) Hot and humid: I was all set to float in the pool and read about three days' worth of newspapers. In all our 17 years here, not once have I had to sit with a newspaper over my head. Where in the hell did that rain come from??

#foolinthepool

4) Puppet making: Matt combined his love of literature/theater with a hobby and made a new puppet today—"Lorca," a Spanish poet. *#cleverkid*

5) Read 20 minutes every day: Well, I will need to read about 3x that much if I think I'll get all these library books read before the due date and renewal period is up! I have not used my library card this much in years as I've done the past 2 months! *#fillmytime #reading #insteadofwritingtop10lists #covid19*

6) Random: I have been through closets and still have a handsome dress suit for a young boy. Please let me know if you know someone who could use it. Van Heusen, size 8. *#free*

7) Pantry challenge: My friend Heidi avoided buying groceries (except for milk and fresh fruit) for one month by using up the staples in the house and meat in the freezer. I was inspired. I used the "Easter ham" that was in the freezer and mixed it in with mac-n-cheese tonight. *#thatsastart*

8) Lipstick: I miss this, but it messes up my masks. You can keep my earrings but give back my lipstick. *#please*

9) No #9, let's skip to #10

#hippety #skippety

10) Signing off: Not quite yet. One more night. Anyone else want to pick up where I leave off?

#nopressure #butsomeoneshould #goforit

What's Next?

Day 101

June 30, 2020

Day 101 ⁓

June 30, 2020

The End: June 30, 2020—Shelter-in-Place/Parallels to the Pandemic

We are at the dead end. The coronavirus continues, but the Top 10 list has run its course. I hope you and your family stay healthy and find things to enjoy despite the COVID-19 restrictions and precautions. Here are some things I am looking forward to:

1) Pedicures.

2) Pool guests.

3) Pool rafts.

4) More sangria.

5) Outdoor dining with friends.

6) Outdoor happy hours.

7) Front room decorating.

8) Kitchen upgrades and colors.

9) Going to bed before 11 p.m.

10) Reading the newspaper on the day it is published.

11) Crazy face coverings and masks.

12) My husband's return to the office.

13) My son's return to work.

14) My daughter's start date for work.

15) My oldest son getting a haircut. (Joe says not a chance!)

16) More weekly road trips with Matt.

17) Posting statuses on Facebook earlier than 10 p.m.

18) Printing pictures from my camera roll.

19) Deleting pictures on my camera roll.

20) Watching for you to create a Top 10 list!

21) And maybe, just maybe, writing another book.

Thanks, again. This has been fun! Stay safe.

#covid19 #theend

(PS: I had wanted to include photos in the book, but my editor said NO! If you are curious to see the images I posted with these lists, please visit my Facebook page at facebook.com/sheri.whiteauthor I would love to engage with you there, too!)

About the Author

Sheri White, retired with a master's degree in Special Education and an Administrative Certificate in Educational Leadership, has worked as a classroom teacher, supported employment specialist, staff development trainer, and program director at an alternative high school and residential program. Sheri has educated thousands of administrators, teachers, school psychologists and social workers on many special education topics. Yes, it was her passion. Since retirement, she has found fun working in the gig economy as a shopper for a major grocery/delivery service.

Sheri learned to look at the ordinary in life and make it into an extraordinary experience every day since her son was diagnosed with a cancerous brain tumor at age two in 1996. She and her husband have raised three children and live in northern Illinois.

This is her first book, one she never planned on writing! Sheri's next book will take a different direction as she writes about the life of her son, Matt, and his journey as a survivor of a cancerous brain tumor.

Connect with Sheri at:

sheriwhiteauthor@gmail.com

www.sheriwhiteauthor.com

www.facebook.com/sheri.whiteauthor

Instagram @white.sherio

Twitter @sheri1006

Sheri is available for speaking engagements, conversation and virtual support to parents who are parenting a child/adult with a disability. And she welcomes your response to this book, *100 Days of Staying the Hell Home in 2020*.